FREEDOM FIGHTERS

The world is waiting for such men.

FREEDOM FIGHTERS

The world is waiting for such men.

JOHN TRIFFITT

In Christ alone.

FREEDOM FIGHTERS – A Training Manual for Men

Copyright © 2019 by John Triffitt.

Published using **Book**Lab services, www.thebooklab.co.uk

No part of this book shall be reproduced or transmitted in any form or by any means, electronic or mechanical, including photocopying, recording, or by any information retrieval system without written permission from the publisher. All photographs are from the authors private collection.

All Bible quotations are from the New King James Version unless otherwise stated in the text.

ISBN: 9781791656058

DEDICATION

This MANual is dedicated to my wife
Paula, Véronique, Natalya and Alex, 'the defender of men'

Thank you for your loving grace
You're the bees' knees and cat's pyjamas

ACKNOWLEDGMENTS

To say this MANual is by 'John Triffitt' is not a true reflection. From my initial first steps in the salvation of Jesus Christ to the path I walk today, many true men have profoundly impacted my life and have shown me the way of the narrow path. I have observed from near and far in these men's lives, homes and ministries what it means to embody the elements of true manhood revealed in and through Jesus Christ. I am eternally grateful for these men pouring out their hearts during the different seasons of my life.

So with much love and special thanks I acknowledge my Dad, Peter Triffitt (for the DNA of no pain no gain, of sweat, blood and tears), Simon Triffitt (the first Triffitt partaker of the life from above), my pastor, Pastor Robert Maasbach (words cannot describe the life of Christ you have consistently imparted to me in love over the past twenty- seven years), Chris Horwood (the man who brought me into his family to live among them), Roy Dufresne (my favourite and only father-in-law; you loved me as a son), Pastor Jack Reid (your resolute love and faith for the unreached is truly humbling), Pastor John Harris (a true shepherd of Christ), Chris Beatton (your love and impact in my life still resounds to this day), Simon Dunsmore (the man who forsakes all for the love of Christ), Ed Robbins (through the highs and the lows, your friendship remains the same), Jason Carter (your gracious heart inspires me to dream), Joel Luce (the angel sent from heaven), Matt Terry (my friend, my brother), Ian Harris (the man in the galley and rowing) and time would fail to tell of Andy Laferme (and his boys), Dave Triffitt, John Cullum, Antony Meade, Martin Dufresne, Simeon Hawkins,

Josh Maasbach, Zach Maasbach, Major Leigh Roberts, Micah Tucker, Laurence Walsh, Giles Cornell, Roger Dufresne, Geoff White, Simon Creasey, Sean England, Stephen Smith, Ben Stringer, Jon Dean, Mark Giles, Mark Price, Michael Blackwell, Philip Symes, Bob Marshall, Pastor Chris Vigil, Dez Bouw, Ali Loaker, Rob Baggaley, Ed Morgan, Dave Brooker, King James, Simon Teague, all the Triff boys (Wez, Ben, Sol and Mal), Pastor John Lowe II, Jim Perry, Darren Winder, Pastor Ron King, Pastor Jeremy Mercer, Tunde Danmole, Chrissy Hilton, Keith Moore, Jason Lock, Eddie Lozano, Josh Townsend, Dan Parrett, Ben Lock, Terence Crompton, Robbin Tyrrell, Marc Giles, Tony Parsons, Tony Betts, John Osborne, Owen Banton, Joe Vargas, Miles Irving, Jez Watkins, Jon Stringer, Sam Lilley, Shayler McCarthy, Rick Hales, George Bettles, Pastor Rob Cooper, Jeff Becker, Pieter Van Rooyen, Andre Torto, Giles Boulton, Wayne Wolstenholme and all those my memory has failed me from naming but a big shout out to all those men who have impacted my life for His Glory.

And finally, much love and appreciation to Virginia Mull (for the outstanding illustrations) and Mark Stibbe, who saw and believed in the message; looking forward to catching up my old pal, and throwing those stones.

CONTENTS

	Acknowledgements	7
1.	KEEPING IT REAL	11
2.	SHARING YOUR TENT	27
3.	KNOWING YOUR ENEMY	41
4.	WEARING YOUR BELT	59
5.	GUARDING YOUR HEART	77
6.	PREPARING YOUR FEET	93
7.	LIFTING YOUR SHIELD	109
8.	PROTECTING YOUR MIND	131
9.	DRAWING YOUR SWORD	147
10.	RAISING A LOUD SHOUT	163

GALEA PECTORALE

BALTEVS SCVTVM

GLADIVS

CALIGAE

CHAPTER 1

KEEPING IT REAL

The Roman Emperor Marcus Aurelius once said, 'let men see, let them know, a real man, who lives as he was meant to live.'

I don't know how you would define a *real man*. There have been many attempts. Thomas Paine once said that 'the real man smiles in trouble, gathers strength from distress, and grows brave by reflection.' Henry Ward Beecher reflected, 'the real man is one who always finds excuses for others but never excuses himself.' More recently, Miranda Hart mused that 'a real man can go out with a woman taller than he is. That's an alpha male right there.'

Many men have tried to summarise what a real man is and all the while women have been waiting. As Chrissie Hinde, lead singer of the band the Pretenders once pleaded, 'Show me a real man now! Where are they?'

Perhaps the clue lies in the word 'real.' Most people think 'real' denotes 'true', as in some supreme model of manhood and masculinity. This usually involves pointing to a particular celebrity - a man who embodies the looks of a George Clooney and the heart of a Denzel Washington. But 'real' can also denote 'open and vulnerable.' It can point to the opposite of 'unreal'. Unreal is false and fictional - characteristics of the cosmetic world of celebrities. It is by definition unreachable. 'Real,' however, is reachable. Real is raw and at the same time redemptive. Real is honest and at the same time hopeful. Real is transparent and at the same time triumphant. Real is the prime characteristic of heroes not celebrities. Real is not touched up or airbrushed. Real is naked truth.

One of the men who played the part of James Bond, Timothy Dalton, said this. 'You can't relate to a superhero, to a superman, but you can identify with a real man who in times of crisis draws strength forth some extraordinary quality from within himself and triumphs, but only after a struggle.' That's right. A real man is not someone who scurries into the phone booth of faith, entering as a beleaguered and bespectacled employee, leaving as a cape-wearing, supersonic champion. A real man is an ordinary man with an extraordinary passion. A real man is an honest, vulnerable male in whom the fire of heaven burns unquenchably.

A real man is quite simply a man who is real.

An Unusual Blessing

A friend of mine was recently teaching at a freedom school in an African American Church. He was talking about the importance of total honesty and transparency in the process of getting free and staying free. He made the point that no one gets free when everyone is trying to be religious but many do in a community where everyone is committed to being real.

He then told a story.

He told of a time when he was asked by the BBC to go into London and answer some questions in a series of interviews about the movie, *The Passion of the Christ*. A taxi driver picked him up at 0500 on a pitch black Sunday morning and drove him to the BBC headquarters. On the way, the taxi driver - a Jamaican guy - asked my friend why he was going to the BBC. This led to a long conversation about the film. The driver had no real understanding of what the Passion involved so it was a great opportunity to share about Jesus.

When the taxi drew up outside Portland House, my friend - feeling that he ought to say something spiritual - gave the man his

CHAPTER 1 | KEEPING IT REAL

fare and a tip and said, 'God bless you.'

The recipient - obviously not used to such early morning benedictions - turned and stammered, 'Uh, okay, keep it real, man.'

My friend reflected afterwards that his blessing was good but the driver's blessing was better. 'Keep it real, man' was a whole lot more challenging. For weeks afterwards, instead of saying 'The Lord bless you' at the end of church services, my friend - who was a pastor - ended with, 'Keep it real.' Being an Anglican church, the congregation responded every time, 'And also with you!'

100 Per Cent

Having told this story, my friend then went on to challenge the attendees at the freedom school to keep it real. He made the point that we all have a choice as Christians today: we can either be religious or we can be real. We can wear masks or we can reveal the face behind the face.

'Religion or reality? That is the question.'

Having finished the talk, an African American man came up to him. He was one of those men who really define 'cool'. He had been a criminal in the underworld in Boston, Massachusetts but then got gloriously saved and wonderfully transformed - a Kingdom gangster, one of God's rough diamonds.

'Hey, do you know what the black kids on the streets are saying these days?'

'I've no idea.'

'They don't use the phrase "keep it real" anymore.'

'What do they say?'

'They say, "Keep it a hunna".'

'What does that mean?'

'Keep it one hundred, as in one hundred per cent.'

My friend looked puzzled.

'They say 'hunna', without pronouncing the d's.'

'Ah, I see.'

From that moment on, the visiting speaker kept on saying this phrase. After five days and nights he had just about mastered both the pronunciation and the concept. The packed class of freedom fighters laughed and clapped every time he said it. At the end, they gave him and his wife two T shirts with 'KEEP IT ONE HUNNA' on them.

'I am the Reality'

Many of us as men don't keep it 100. We don't live with our masks off, communicating at the deepest level with our spouses or friends. We find it hard to open up, to be authentic. We have an innate fear of vulnerability. We are supposed to be strong - hunters, fighters, explorers, pioneers, protectors, adventurers, warriors and gatherers. We are not supposed to show weakness. 'Big boys don't cry.' That's what we're told. So we cover up and all the while we do, our freedom becomes more and more elusive.

There was once a man who kept it real. His name was Jesus. He was 100 per cent real every moment of his life. He never wore a mask, never pretended to be someone he wasn't. In fact, He went around criticising those who wore masks, especially His religious contemporaries. He told the ultra-religious men of His day that they were 'hypocrites', a word that originally referred to actors who wore masks on the stages of Greek and Roman theatres. Jesus was crystal clear. Religion means 'masks on.' Reality means 'masks off.'

Why do you think the most flawed and fractured people of His day felt so comfortable in His presence? Why do you think prostitutes and sinners felt they were welcome at the Messiah's meals? It was because Jesus was real not religious. It was because they knew He was an exceptional, accepting, loving man. He was

CHAPTER 1 | KEEPING IT REAL

the Son of Man - man as He was created to be. Here was a man who held banquets for the broken. Here was a man who understood what it was to be despised, rejected, homeless and poor and yet who had a heart free from bitterness and violence. Here was a real man - a man who loved reality and hated religion.

Jesus never hid what he was really feeling.

When His Passion was approaching - His suffering and death on a hill far away - He openly stated that His soul was troubled and in Gethsemane He was so stressed by the prospect of His imminent crucifixion that He sweated blood.

A few days earlier, He went into the Temple and threw a fit, turning over tables and whipping the money-changers. You've heard of road rage and air rage. This is when people get enraged when they're in cars or airplanes. Well this was religion rage - extreme anger at the way people had turned the Father's house into a place of religious exploitation.

A few days before that, Jesus went to the funeral of a friend. When He saw his mate's tomb, He stood outside and fell to pieces. John 11:35 is the shortest verse in the Bible, just two words: 'Jesus wept.' The word 'wept' is loaded. Many of the bystanders were crying. John uses a different word to describe their tears - a word suggesting that they were professional mourners. The word John uses for Jesus' tears is wholly different. It means that He sobbed.

These were no crocodile tears.

Jesus' eyes were red and His face was wet because He was 100 per cent.

You get the point?

Jesus didn't wear a mask.

He wore His heart on His sleeve.

He was transparent and vulnerable.

He was completely real.

Facing the Music

Why is 'being 100' so important? Jesus answers the question. To those who chose to continue following Him, he told them that they would know the truth and the truth would set them free (John 8:31-32). Is your heart stirred by that promise?

Do you long to be a man who is completely free - free from the sins that entangle, free from the wounds that bind you, the shame that hinders, the rejection that lingers, the addictions that threaten to destroy your manhood, your marriage, your work, your ministry?

Here's the answer. 'You shall know the truth.'

What does that mean?

In the original language of the New Testament, the word that Jesus uses is aletheia. This is an amazing word. To our ancestors it meant, 'reality.' What mattered most was discovering what was ultimately real - what lay behind the surface of things, beyond the world of pretence and shadows.

Here's what Jesus' promise sounds like when we use this word. 'You shall know reality and what's really real will set you free.'

That's stunning. Our freedom as men comes not from being superficial but from being transparent. When we decide to face the music, even when we don't like the tune, Jesus starts to set us free from the destructive patterns of our lives - the cycles of thinking and behaving that threaten to rob us of our peace and steal away our destiny.

Wouldn't you like to be truly free?

Then you and I have to be really real! As the Nike slogan says. 'Just do it.'

You know what nike means in Greek? It means 'victory.'

If we want to be champions, we need to be real, to see things as

CHAPTER 1 | KEEPING IT REAL

they really are.

The good news is that we don't need to do this alone.

We can do it with Jesus, the man who defined reality, the man who said, 'I am the Way, the Reality and the Life' (John 14:6).

Free and Forgiven

As men, we are called to get free and stay free. That's what it means to be a true man of God. The Bible makes it abundantly clear that those who choose to follow Jesus choose to follow the One who sets us free. That's why the apostle John tells us that 'he whom the Son sets free is free indeed.' That's why another man who underwent a profound transformation, the apostle Paul, was adamant that 'it is for freedom that Christ has set us free.'

Don't just settle for being forgiven.

Enjoy your freedom too!

The sad fact is that too many men are forgiven but not free.

As men we need to learn to fight for our freedom. We need to be active not passive in getting free and staying free. This is part of our inheritance as the adopted sons of God. We are called to be freedom fighters, not only fighting for our own freedom but for the freedom of other men too. Our freedom is too good to be kept to ourselves. We are to walk in our freedom and give it away. We are to get free and then set others free.

As the saying goes, free people set people free.

Hurting people just end up hurting people.

As men we are called to fight daily to keep and indeed to share the freedom that Christ won at the Cross. The whole of creation is waiting for men like this. The planet is pining for the revelation of the sons of God - for the appearance on the earth of men who truly know what it is to be set free from the downward pull of sin and death, men who are upwardly mobile in the aerodynamic lift of the Spirit's power. This is the Spirit that raised Jesus from the dead and lifted Him high into the Heavenly realms, where He sits with His Father in glory. The Spirit has infinite, immense, incomparable power. It's grave-busting and death-defeating power. It is the kind of power that cuts through chains like a red hot blade through butter. When we fight for freedom we have God on our side.

Exposing the Shadows

The secret is to start with our own lives. As men, we need to understand that we are not going to lead anyone else until we have learned to lead ourselves. No one can manage another man until they have learned to manage their own hearts. This means being ruthlessly honest. We need to let the Holy Spirit go into the deepest parts of our souls and expose the darkness.

If you've ever had a bowel scan you'll know that this can be a little uncomfortable! You have to lie on your side on a gurney with your bare backside facing a surgeon and his team, some of whom may be women. A probe is inserted with a camera and a bright light on the front end. This then travels up your lower bowel and sometimes further, transmitting images onto a screen.

Yes, you guessed right. Your innards are on prime time TV.

'There's a tiny polyp,' the surgeon will sometimes say.

'Where?' you ask, straining your misty eyes towards the monitor.

'That tiny shadow, right there… we'll remove that and send it to be examined.'

The next moment the shadow's gone and you're onto the next excision.

As men we need to learn to let the Great Physician have access to our innermost being and shine His light onto those parts of our secret world that need His expert surgery. We all have shadows in our lives. Our shadows are the hurts, habits and hang-ups that

CHAPTER 1 | KEEPING IT REAL

we try to keep concealed. Left unchecked, they could develop into something really destructive.

A true man of God allows the Holy Spirit to shine His light on even the most hidden parts of our personalities. A real man repeats the prayer of one of the Bible's real men - King David. He says,

Search me, God, and know my heart;
test me and know my anxious thoughts.
See if there is any offensive way in me,
and lead me in the way everlasting. Psalm 139:23-24

A real man says with the Apostle John,

If we claim to have fellowship with him and yet walk in the darkness, we lie and do not live out the truth. But if we walk in the light, as he is in the light, we have fellowship with one another, and the blood of Jesus, his Son, purifies us from all sin. 1 John 1:6-7

True men bring harmful hurts, habits and hang-ups into the open.

True men walk in the light.

True men fight for the light.

Heaven's Weapons

In this book I am going to use many of the insights from the book I co-authored with Mark Stibbe - *Behold the Man. Jesus Christ and True Masculinity*. There I underlined the fact that the New Testament was written when Rome ruled the world. The Romans had a clear idea of what constituted a manly man and that image was modelled by their Emperor. Then Jesus entered history. He introduced a whole new image of what a real man looks like - a man who embodied the values of the Kingdom of God not the Empire of Rome. This man, not Caesar, is the true image of both masculinity and manhood. If you and I want to be real men - men who embrace the core value of being real - then we need look no further than

Jesus. It is Christ not Caesar who defines what a man should really look like. It is Jesus Christ, not the celebrity males whom the world champions, who defines what a man should really look like.

So how, in practical terms, can this be achieved?

This is where the New Testament's most famous Roman citizen comes to our aid - no, not Pilate but Paul.

Paul not only grew up in the Roman Empire. He also had the priceless status of a Roman citizen. He was therefore very familiar with Roman culture and customs, as his letters in the New Testament reveal. In particular, Paul was used to the sound of the marching feet of the Roman legions. He was accustomed to the glint and glare of the breastplates and helmets of the Roman legionaries. Paul lived at a time when the Roman war machine was making its way across the globe, enforcing what was known as *Pax Romana* - Rome's idea of peace - on foreign lands and barbarian hordes.

Paul saw all that and, under the inspired creativity of the Holy Spirit, called Christians to become heaven's legionaries. He used the picture of the Roman soldier and called us to put on God's armour. Each piece of this holy armour stands for something that enables men to live in the freedom that Jesus won for us at a great price when He died at the hands of Roman soldiers on Calvary's hill. These pieces stand for the values of another world - the ethos and the ethics of the Kingdom of heaven. Those who put on these pieces of armour will not only stay free. They will bring freedom to others. This freedom is not like the peace of Rome - a cessation of hostilities brought about through the violent subjugation of others. This is the peace of God - a peace that the world cannot give. This peace does not deprive a person of their freedom. It releases them into the glorious freedom of the children of God!

In this book I'm going to go through these items of armour one by one, unpacking what each means in a far more practical way than I did in *Behold the Man*. This is not a theoretical book. This is a training manual designed to equip freedom fighters, men of war who fight with weapons that represent the complete opposite of the blood-thirsty and terror-inducing tactics of this world. These are weapons that are rooted in God's love not in man's blood lust. They are subversive, heavenly, and peace loving.

They are everything we need to stay free and bring freedom to others.

Freedom fighters come heavily armed for the battle!

The Warrior Spirit

So being a real man means being a warrior.

It means being a freedom fighter - fighting for our own freedom and for the freedom of those whom we influence.

It means being like Jesus.

As I shared at the start of this chapter, the Roman Emperor Marcus Aurelius once said, 'let men see, let them know, a real man, who lives as he was meant to live.'

We have seen it.

History has given us a glimpse.

Pilate, a champion of Rome's misguided idea of masculinity, snatched a sneak preview.

The one real man worth emulating was not sitting on a comfortable throne in Rome but preparing to climb an excruciating throne at Golgotha.

He was standing right in front of Pilate.

Jesus is the one consistently real man in history. That is why an intuitive cry rose up from deep within the Roman governor's soul, 'BEHOLD, THE MAN!'

Jesus is our inspiration. As men we can be shaped so that more and more we look like Him, think like Him, walk like Him, talk like Him and behave like Him.

The whole world is waiting for such men.

Wives are waiting.

Sons and daughters are waiting.

Orphans and widows are waiting.

Troubled teens are waiting.

Slaves and refugees are waiting.

Let the real men arise!

Let the freedom fighters break out of religion and embrace reality.

CHAPTER 1 | KEEPING IT REAL

APPLYING THE FREEDOM FIGHTING PRINCIPLES

What am I going to *do* in response to what I've read in this chapter?

Action Point 1

Action Point 2

Action Point 3

What am I going to pray for as a result of what I've read?

Prayer Point 1

Prayer Point 2

Prayer Point 3

PERSONAL TRAINING:

The Roman Emperor Marcus Aurelius once said, 'let men see, let them know, a real man, who lives as he was meant to live.'

Consider ways in which Jesus was real rather than religious.

Make a list of ten things you love about the way Jesus modelled what it means to be a real man - a man who's real - and then ask Jesus for each of these qualities or virtues for yourself.

The Virtues of a Real Man (as seen in Jesus)

- _____
- _____
- _____
- _____
- _____
- _____
- _____
- _____
- _____
- _____

Now pray for these in your own life

CHAPTER 1 | KEEPING IT REAL

GROUP TRAINING:

Gather a few Christian men, maybe at a pub or around at your house, and start a discussion on the issues raised in the box below.

Could you use this initial conversation as a springboard for getting other men to read this book and start a Freedom Fighter's group?

- **What does it mean for a man to be 'real' these days?**

- **How tough is it for men to be vulnerable with other men?**

- **Why is that?**

- **Where is it toughest for us to be real?**

- **What would make it easier to be transparent?**

- **What's it going to take for us to remove our masks and be free to be?**

- **What can we do from here?**

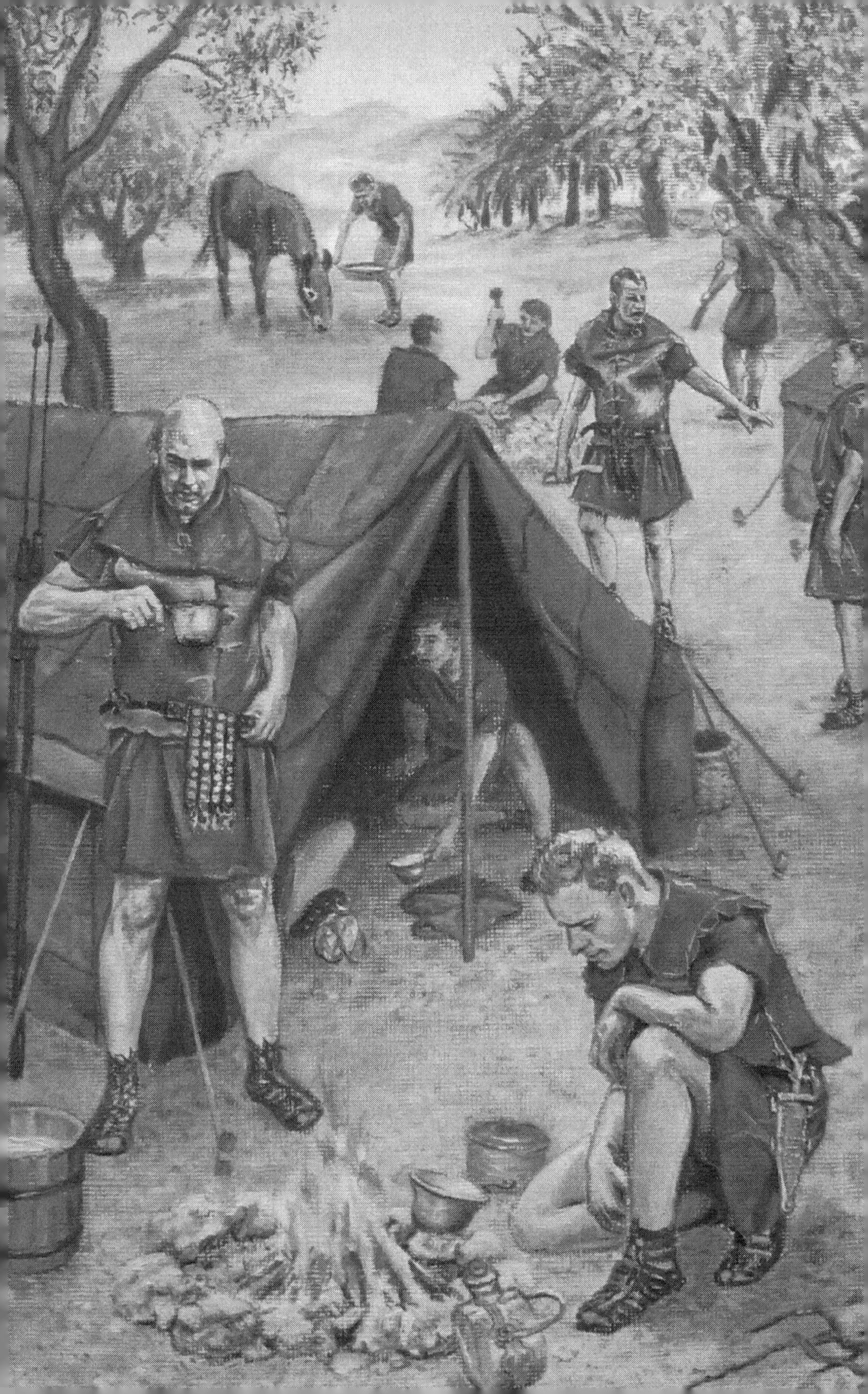

CHAPTER 2

SHARING YOUR TENT

When was the last time you shared a tent with a group of men? Was it an exhilarating experience? Or was it a disaster?

If you've been in the Regular or the Territorial Army, or you've spent some time as a cadet, you will no doubt have some stories to tell, of orienteering through mountain ranges, streams and valleys, taking a breather on some mossy hill, before making your way exhausted towards a destination or a target.

Above all, you will have some tales to tell of nights spent sleeping under canvas with the sound of snoring and the rancid odour of unwashed armpits and sweaty feet.

You will tell a tale of deprivation, yes, but you will also carry a memory of solidarity, of brotherhood in arms, for the rest of your life.

If you've never experienced this, maybe you've been on holiday and slept inside a sleeping bag, listening to the sound of the canvas flapping in the wind, the patter of the rain on the roof of your tent, tasting for a moment what it's like to live rough and in the wild.

Maybe you've been to a camp with other boys and told stories and jokes into the small hours of the morning, muffling your laughter with your hands.

All of us have been tent dwellers at some point or other in our lives, even if one night was more than enough to put us off.

Living under Canvas

Every boy grows up with a basic knowledge of the greatest war machine the world has ever seen. I'm talking about the Roman Army that marched from Rome throughout the world, imposing order on the globe, enforcing worship of the Roman Emperor on every tribe and nation on the earth. Every boy knows that the secret to this war machine was the Roman legion - a unit of just under six thousand men. If they have listened well at school, they will also know that the legion was then divided into ten cohorts of nearly 600 men, and that each cohort was further broken down into six centuries of, yes you guessed it, roughly one hundred men - led, of course, by a centurion. All this is common knowledge.

But did you know that every century was further broken down into smaller units?

Did you know that these ten-man groups spent their entire service together, night and day, both near to Rome and in the furthest reaches of the Empire?

Did you know what this fundamental unit was called?

I'll tell you.

It was called the *contubernium* and it formed the basic building block of the Roman army throughout history.

The word *contubernium* refers to sharing a tent together. This tent had room for about eight men. It was about 3 metres square, and about 1.5 metres tall. It was made entirely of leather and carried on the march by a pack mule. This mule was led and tended by a slave. It carried not only the tent but the two poles, the ropes, baskets, digging tools, a stone wheat grinder and food. When the Roman army camped for the night, these tents would be placed so close together that no enemy would be able to forge a path between them.

Six soldiers would sleep at a time during the watches of the night. The other two would be on guard. This meant that a small

CHAPTER 2 | SHARING YOUR TENT

amount of space was available for the soldiers' belongings and equipment, such as their digging tools. Their shields and spears would be stacked outside the entrance of the tent. These could be picked up at a moment's notice if an attack against the camp was launched.

The tent covered an area of nearly 20 square metres and weighed almost 18 kilograms. Its leather was made up of thirty four panels, each one 40 millimetres thick. The material was made of calf or goat skin.

Small is Beautiful

The word *contubernium* is a combination of two words. The first is con which means 'together'. The second is *taberna* which was originally the name for a military tent - so-called because it was made up of leather boards or panels known as *tabulae*.

Why was the *conturbernium* such an effective unit on which to build an army? The answer is because these eight men knew each other well. They knew each others' strengths and weaknesses. They trained together and they fought together. They ate together and they slept together. They laughed together and they wept together.

These men were known as the *conturbernales* - tent sharers. They were led by the oldest, most experienced legionary in the group. He was known as the *decanus* and he had a rank equivalent to that of a non-commissioned officer. He was also referred to as caput *contubernalii*, the head of the tent sharers. These leaders supervised the setting up and taking down of the tent and they maintained discipline among the *conturbernes*. In addition, they were in charge of the slave who looked after the mule and the slave who looked after the men. These two slaves, known as calones, had many duties. They had to provide water and food for the legionaries and use carpentry skills to make repairs. The number of the *conturbernes* was therefore ten in all - seven soldiers, one *decanus*, and two slaves.

No one seems to have understood better than the Romans

how important such a small group of men can be to the success of a much larger force. If the focus had been on the legion of six thousand men, the Roman army would have been far less efficient and effective. But it was not. The focus was on the eight men that shared a tent. These men, under attack, would close ranks and defend each other to the death. They would charge and roar as one when moving from defence into offence, marching side by side towards the enemy, watching out for one another, ready to raise their huge shields to cover a fellow tent mate if an unseen spear or arrow made its way towards him.

The secret of the success of the Roman army lay therefore lay in its 600 units of tent dwellers. Each man looked out for the others in the tent. Each one effectively said to his comrade, "I've got your back."

Who's got your back?

Unity and Loyalty

Even though these tent dwellers formed a group of diverse men they were utterly united in their cause, even while being different in their experience and skills.

Most notable was the diversity of age. In every *contubernium*, there would have been a veteran of many campaigns and he was usually the non-commissioned officer in charge - the *decanus*, meaning 'chief of ten'. He would have seen many battles and his dream was to survive twenty five years of service until he could hang up his sword and retire in a villa in some idyllic plot of land, given to him by the Emperor. His role was to impart the wisdom of his considerable experience to the younger men, encouraging them when they were fearful or weary, chastising them when they were out of line or unruly.

In stark contrast were the new recruits, usually much younger and without experience. These men came into the *contubernium* every time the group had lost men through death, injury or

CHAPTER 2 | SHARING YOUR TENT

retirement. These new recruits would fill the spaces left by the departed *conturbernales*, completing the compliment of eight legionaries and two auxiliaries.

In every group of ten there was accordingly a diversity of ages, from young men of about 17, through men in their thirties, to men in their mid forties nearing retirement.

Then there was secondly a diversity of responsibilities. New recruits would take up fatigue duties such as stone breaking, filling and boiling kettles, latrine cleaning and stoking the furnace. As they proved faithful in those manual chores and duties, they would then move on to more specialised tasks. These would be allocated in line with the gifts they displayed in the apprentice phase. Some of these involved being stone masons, surveyors, trumpeters, clerks and huntsmen. As the *decanus* observed their conduct early on, he would identify what their strengths were and seek to maximise those for the benefit of the unit.

So there was a diversity of skills as well as age.

In spite of this, these men were bound together by their loyalty to the Emperor and to the General in command of the legion. Every one of the tent sharers had sworn allegiance to Caesar. This oath was known as the *sacramentum militari* and took the following form:

'The soldiers swear that they shall faithfully execute all that the Emperor commands, that they shall never desert the service, and that they shall not seek to avoid death for the Roman Republic.'

What bound them together was therefore more spiritual than physical. Yes there were similarities in the physical appearance of the Roman legionary. This was less to do with height and more to do with strength. Flavius Vegetius Renatus underlines the point:

"Let, therefore, the youth who is to be chosen for martial tasks have observant eyes, hold his head up, have a broad chest, muscular shoulders, strong arms, long fingers, not too extended a waist measure, lean hams, and calves and feet not distended with superfluous flesh but hard and knotted with muscles. Whenever you find these marks in the recruit, do not be troubled about his height. It is more useful for soldiers to be strong and brave than big."

But the common denominator for all the *conturbanales* was the fact they were fiercely loyal to their Emperor, the one whom they addressed and worshipped as "Lord" and "God", "Saviour of the World", "Bringer of Peace," even "Son of God."

The Only Son of God

For Christian men from the time of the New Testament onwards, there is only one man in history who deserves those titles. There is only one man who has been worthy of heart-felt worship and the highest praise.

I'm talking about Jesus.

Jesus didn't sit on a throne in Rome, ruling the world through the love of power. He hung upon a Cross at Golgotha and rules the world today through the power of love.

Jesus didn't coerce the world into experiencing peace. He invited every tribe and nation to enjoy a peace that the world cannot give.

To Christian men, Jesus alone is Lord.

Jesus alone is worthy of being revered and worshipped as God.

Jesus alone is truly the Saviour of the World.

Jesus alone is the Prince of Peace and the Bringer of Peace.

Jesus alone is the Son of the Living God.

For Christian men in the first century, and for Christian men in the twenty first century, our worship can never be directed towards a human emperor, president, prime minister or monarch. The Emperors of Rome demanded that they were adored as gods. In effect, they made themselves into deities and insisted that all citizens bowed down and worshipped them, burning incense and declaring that 'Caesar is Lord.' For Christian men this is unthinkable. The

CHAPTER 2 | SHARING YOUR TENT

Emperors were not deserving of such adulation. Without exception their morality was questionable at best. Furthermore, they were some among the many men in history who've sought to become gods. Jesus was the exact opposite. He is the only example in history of God seeking to become man. He is therefore the only one who deserves to be called 'Son of God' and 'Lord.' He did not exalt himself in pride, allowing others to treat him as divine. He humbled himself. As the Apostle Paul proclaimed:

Let this mind be in you which was also in Christ Jesus, who, being in the form of God, did not consider it robbery to be equal with God, but made Himself of no reputation, taking the form of a bondservant, and coming in the likeness of men. And being found in appearance as a man, He humbled Himself and became obedient to the point of death, even the death of the cross. Therefore God also has highly exalted Him and given Him the name which is above every name, that at the name of Jesus every knee should bow, of those in heaven, and of those on earth, and of those under the earth, and that every tongue should confess that Jesus Christ is Lord, to the glory of God the Father.

It took a real man to say that in the first century, when the rule of the Emperor extended everywhere.

It took a real man to declare, 'Jesus is Lord. Caesar is not!'

You're in the Army Now

If Christian men are to be real men, then they cannot live the Christian life alone. Following Jesus is no simple, cost-free call. It is a life that costs you everything. It is like joining an army. It is volunteering to fight the good fight against an enemy so ruthless that no earthly terrorist or tyrant can compare with him. If that is really the case, and the Bible tells us it is, then we would be foolish to fight alone. We need each other.

So many men of us forget this. We think we can survive on our own. Bowing without realising it to the idol of individualism, so rampant in our culture, we seek to manage our lives on our own, without the support of other men, without accountability. This is weakness not strength. Seeking to navigate through life without recourse to others is the very pinnacle of weakness because it is the very essence of folly. No man can fight alone. No man can win against a cruel, malicious enemy without the help of other men. We need each other. We need to fight together. We need to stand together. We need to raise the freedom flag in companies of other men not all alone on some high and isolated hill.

Too many men have believed the lie that they can go it alone. Too many men, good men, have left churches feeling that their local church does not equip, support and nourish them. Too many have left churches altogether, maybe as a result of disappointment or a feeling of rejection. Too many men have become part of the great, disorganised and largely dormant army of the 'dechurched' as they're called - those who used to be a part but now are more apart from communities of Jesus-loving followers. This is not only dangerous. It's such a dreadful waste of vital gifts and callings.

Are you one of those men?

Are you living the Christian life alone?

If you are, remember this truth - Jesus integrates but the devil isolates.

The devil wants to get us on our own. When we are all alone we become an easy target. His arrows reach us without any warning. One day we are doing well. The next day we have fallen wounded in a battle we could easily have won had we been part of a band of brothers looking out for us, calling us into a love-based lifestyle of accountability.

As Christian men we need to understand a truth that is vital not only to our survival in the battle, but to our victory as well.

We need our *contubernium*.

We need to be a part of a vibrant group of freedom fighters.

We need committed brothers who can watch our backs.

CHAPTER 2 | SHARING YOUR TENT

Standing Together

Pretty well every Christian man will know the passage in Ephesians 6 where the Apostle Paul talks about the armour of God. I want you to read it again right now but read it with a different set of spectacles. Take off your cultural spectacles. They come from the world's way of seeing things. They come from a culture that has lost the value of community, where families and whole societies have lost togetherness and fractured into many isolated parts. Take off these glasses. They will not help you. They cannot.

Instead, I urge you to put on your kingdom spectacles. In the Kingdom of heaven, family is everything. In heaven, God is three persons yet one being. He is three in one and one in three. He is family - an eternal, ever-loving family of Father, Son and Holy Spirit. Everything about the kingdom shouts "family". In the kingdom of heaven, there is no such thing as a solitary, individualistic love for Jesus. Yes we are called to have a *personal* faith, but *personal* does not mean going it alone. In the kingdom, men are supposed to help each other.

So put on your kingdom spectacles. Look at what the Apostle Paul is saying. He is telling you to do something. But when he says 'you', he does not mean 'you individually'. He means 'you collectively'. The word 'you' in this passage is plural not singular. It means all of you, or what our American brothers sometimes call Y'ALL!

My brethren, be strong in the Lord and in the power of His might. Put on the whole armour of God, that you may be able to stand against the wiles of the devil. For we do not wrestle against flesh and blood, but against principalities, against powers, against the rulers of the darkness of this age, against spiritual hosts of wickedness in the heavenly places. Therefore take up the whole armour of God, that you may be able to withstand in the evil day, and having done all, to stand.

Stand therefore, having girded your waist with truth, having put on the breastplate of righteousness, and having shod your feet with the preparation of the gospel of peace; above all, taking the shield of faith with which you will be able to quench all the fiery darts of the wicked one. And take the helmet of salvation, and the sword of the Spirit, which is the word of God; praying always with all prayer and supplication in the Spirit, being watchful to this end with all perseverance and supplication for all the saints.

Do you see the difference it makes when we see 'you' as plural not as singular? Paul is addressing 'brethren.' That's a plural word. That's a group. That's many men, not just one. It's legions of men, not individual legionaries.

Paul is saying no to independence and yes to interdependence.

If we are to be freedom fighters in this world, fighting for our own freedom and the freedom of the many others whom we influence, then we need each other. We need as men to put on the whole armour of God together. We need to have a common understanding of our enemy and his insidious and cruel tactics. We need to stand firm and we need to stand together.

We need our *contubernium*.

We need each other.

So, my friends, it's time to make and set up a tent. It's time to find other men to share it. It's time to become a group of freedom fighters.

Will you join a *contubernium* of brothers who have got your back?

Will you swear an oath of lifelong loyalty to Jesus Christ?

Will you help each other to put your armour on?

Will you stand with other brothers in the furious battle for the freedom of our planet?

Will you bring your gifts to a group of men, believing that no one man has got it all together, but that altogether you've got it?

APPLYING THE FREEDOM FIGHTING PRINCIPLES

What am I going to *do* in response to what I've read in this chapter?

Action Point 1

Action Point 2

Action Point 3

What am I going to pray for as a result of what I've read?

Prayer Point 1

Prayer Point 2

Prayer Point 3

PERSONAL TRAINING:

Spend some time considering the questions in the box and bring these to the Lord in prayer.

WHERE IS MY TENT?

- **Am I already part of a group of Christian men?**

- **If so, how can I apply the teaching of this chapter in that group and take things to another level?**

- **If not, are there men in my world whom I could invite to form a *conturbernium*?**

- **What can I do to become less independent and more interdependent?**

- **Who are the men I'm going to stand with in the future?**

CHAPTER 2 | SHARING YOUR TENT

GROUP TRAINING:

As you form into a group of about ten men, consider how you might consolidate your commitment to the freedom fighter's cause by making an oath of allegiance to the Lord and to each other. Use the following to express your dedication:

THE FREEDOM FIGHTER'S OATH OF ALLEGIANCE:

As Christian men we pledge our heart's allegiance to our Lord and Saviour, Jesus Christ. We believe that He is God and no one else and that one day every knee will bow and every tongue confess that Jesus Christ is Lord. Until that glorious day, we now declare that we will serve Him with undying loyalty. We decree that we will serve each other, guard each others' backs and help each other in the battle as we stand as one against the enemy. As freedom fighters for the King of Kings, we make our oath today and say, "Set us free, Lord Jesus and through us set our families and nation free!"

Offer a loud shout unto the Lord when you're done

Think of using this oath every time a man joins the group

Maybe use it on the anniversary of the formation of your groups

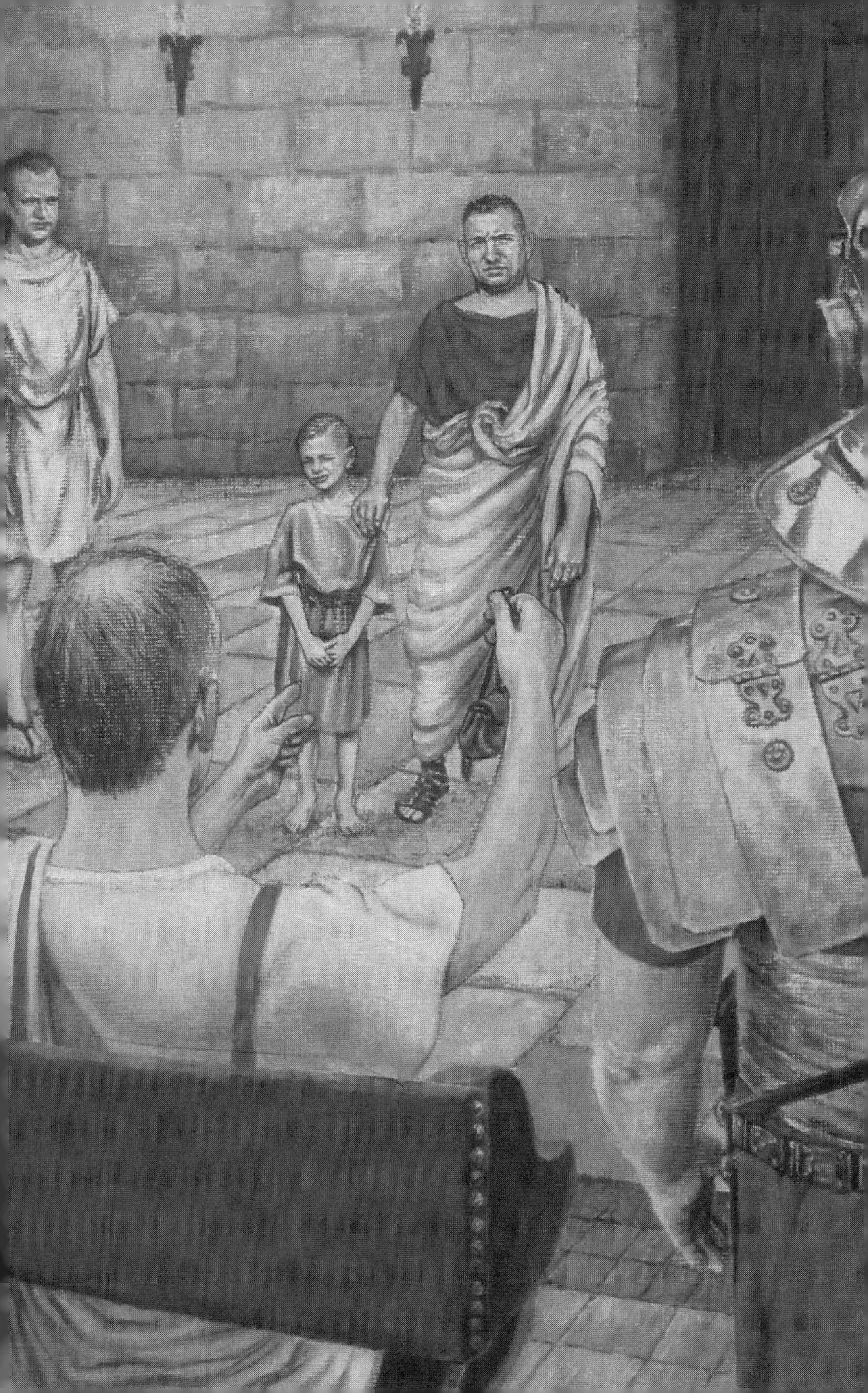

CHAPTER 3

KNOWING YOUR ENEMY

A picture, it is said, is worth a thousand words. Sometimes you need to see a picture before you can appropriate a truth.

So let me present a picture. It's a picture that the Apostle Paul has in mind in his letters. On five occasions he uses a word that evoked a clear and powerful picture in the minds of the first readers of his letters. The word is "adoption."

Let me paint the picture.

Let me tell you the story.

It is fictional. At the same time, it is the sort of scenario that Paul had in mind.

It is the first century AD and a boy called Publius grows up as the son of a slave. He and his father and mother, along with his younger brother and sister, are slaves in the household of a Roman merchant who lives just outside Rome. The master is rich; he has everything that he could possibly want in life except for one thing - a son. He and his wife are childless, something which, in Roman society, is feared. He and his wife cannot have children and they are now desperately worried about whether or not they are going to be able to continue the so-called *pater familias* - the family line on the husband's side.

One day Publius, who is now seven years old, overhears a conversation between his father and his Master.

"I have a question," the Master says.

"What is it, Master?"

"Would you like your boy Publius to grow up to be a free man?"

"Yes, Master, more than anything."

"Then why don't you let me adopt him as my son."

Publius is about to gasp out loud but covers his mouth just in time.

"Think of it," the Master continues. "Your son will grow up free, no longer prone to the dangers and deprivations of a slave. His debts will be cancelled. He will be the sole inheritor of all that I and my family have built."

Publius peers through the latticed partition and sees his Master stretching out an arm to encompass the great villa, its walled grounds and the vineyards beyond.

"He can do anything he likes once he is older. He can run the family business. He can go into the senate. He can join the army. He will be free to choose a profession that he loves rather than live under a yoke that he hates."

The Master pauses.

"He will have a future and a hope," he concludes.

Publius' father strokes his chin for a second.

"It's a good question," he says.

Several days later, Publius travels into town and stands with his father before a magistrate. His father has told him that his life is going to change forever and there have been tears as the time draws near. Publius has held tightly to his mother, relishing every final touch, every scent. Now he is with his father, holding his hand one last time, suppressing the sob within.

"Begin the sale," the magistrate intones.

CHAPTER 3 | KNOWING YOUR ENEMY

Three times Publius is passed from his father to his Master and each time his Master places a bag of coins before the Magistrate. After the third time, his father picks up the money and thrusts it in a bag he is carrying over his shoulder.

"Sold!" the magistrate declares. "This boy," he adds, "is free. From this moment on, he is the son of this new father. He is the heir of the estate. He has all the rights of sonship. He is no longer a slave. All his debts are hereby cancelled."

With that, Publius watches his father turn to leave. After he has walked away, Publius looks up. His new father has kind eyes and a warm smile.

"My son," he sighs, a single tear falling down his sun-tanned face. "My precious, darling son, welcome to the family."

The Master lifts his arms and drapes it over Publius shoulder, the folds of a white toga covering his back, trembling in the breeze.

"I have the rest of the day off," the father says. "I am going to take you on a chariot around the estate and you're going to see what's now yours."

A Life of Freedom

That was a story that played out thousands and thousands of times in the era of the Apostle Paul. Paul was a Roman citizen so he knew that this was a familiar tale. He may have seen it acted out in market places across the Roman Empire where the sons of slaves were purchased out of slavery by childless men. In Latin it was known as *adoptio*. In Greek, the language in which the New Testament was written, it was known as *huiothesia*, which means "the act of giving someone the position of a son."

In Paul's day, this practice of adoption was very common. Paul was operating in a patriarchal or male-centred society. It was therefore normally a son that was adopted. What mattered to the Romans was having a boy so that the family line could be perpetuated. Being childless meant the shame of a discontinued lineage as opposed to the honour of a noble heritage. In Roman society, adopting the son of a slave was an obvious way round this dilemma. There were boys like Publius everywhere.

To us today, with our very different ways of adopting children, the actual practice may seem strange. While we may be able to see the advantages to the new father, it may be hard for us to understand why the biological dad and mum would have ever wanted to let their children go. But what we must remember is that there was no life more precarious in the Roman Empire than the life of a slave. Slaves were in constant peril and their days were marked by constant servitude and drudgery, with little hope of ever finding freedom.

For Publius and those like him, adoption was like winning the lottery. Yes there was grief in the goodbyes but there was also joy in what lay ahead. After the legal rite performed by the magistrate, the boy could now expect a life of freedom and a future fortune with it. He was now declared the "actual son and heir" of his new father. He was now under a new father's authority - a father that wanted the best for him and was able to give him the best, whatever that boy dreamed and desired.

For the new son, therefore, adoption meant moving from existing to living.

It meant an end to the state of being a slave.

It meant an end to poverty.

It meant a beginning to freedom.

What a Great Picture!

This is an amazing analogy - a stunning image that Paul discovered of what Christ has done for us. Before we met Jesus, we were slaves. We lived a life of bondage to sin and death. We were under the authority of Satan, the father of lies. We were tied to

CHAPTER 3 | KNOWING YOUR ENEMY

him, always bound and bitterly restricted by his heavy chains. We had no way out. Our lives lacked hope and purpose. We were in a desperate, perilous state.

But then a father said, "I want to adopt you." This father was no ordinary dad. He was and is the God and Father of our Lord Jesus Christ - the world's greatest Dad, the universe's perfect Father. He cried from heaven, "No more orphans! No more slaves! I want to set the captives free."

So He sent His one and only Son, Jesus Christ, into the world and on the Cross paid the price for our redemption, for our freedom from a life of slavery. He paid it not with bags of gold and silver but with the precious blood of Jesus, shed for us on Calvary's hill.

When He had done what we could never do, the price was paid and we were free.

All we had to do was repent of sin and put our trust in Jesus Christ and we could live each day with all the privileges of our adoption.

We could become receivers of the glorious freedom of the children of God.

We could become the beneficiaries of the incomparable riches of heaven.

We could become debt free as far as all our previous sins were concerned.

We could become heirs of our Heavenly Father's estate, one day inheriting the earth!

We could become the sons of the Most High God, no longer living under the authority of the father of lies but under the authority of the Father of Lights.

We could become soldiers in the army of God, fighting for the Kingdom of Light, breaking the chains of those held captive by the enemy.

We could become freedom fighters, bringing others in our world into the glorious freedom that we now enjoy.

We could become the answer to this dying planet, groaning as it is in eager longing for the revelation, the appearance, of the sons of God.

From Slavery to Sonship

By now, some of you may be asking, "Where is all this in the Bible?" There are five passages where Paul uses the word "adoption" and in which he explores this picture of the slave who turns into a perfect Father's son and heir. Let's look at two.

Paul makes it clear that our loving Heavenly Father purposed right from the very beginning of history that one day He would adopt us as his sons. Here is Ephesians 1:3-6:

Blessed be the God and Father of our Lord Jesus Christ, who has blessed us with every spiritual blessing in the heavenly places in Christ, just as He chose us in Him before the foundation of the world, that we should be holy and without blame before Him in love, having predestined us to adoption as sons by Jesus Christ to Himself, according to the good pleasure of His will, to the praise of the glory of His grace, by which He made us accepted in the Beloved.

If you're a man of God, walking by faith in Jesus, then you are one of those that God the Father predestined to become his adopted sons.

What a privilege!

What an honour!

Even when Adam and Eve sinned, our Father had a backup plan. He had already decided that He would not let us stay in slavery to an orphan state. He knew that Jesus would one day pay the price and break the chains. He knew that one day we would look up into His smiling face and call Him "Father". This was not just His decision. It was His delight. It brought Him everlasting pleasure! If you've received your adoption certificate from heaven, you can now rest from the servitude of trying to measure up to God's requirements, the slavery of always striving to earn His approval. You are now "accepted in the Beloved!"

Then, to mention just one other Scripture passage, there is Galatians 4:4-7:

When the fullness of the time had come, God sent forth His Son, born of a woman, born under the law, to redeem those who were under the law, that we might receive the adoption as sons. And because you are sons, God has sent forth the Spirit of His Son into your hearts, crying out, "Abba, Father!" Therefore you are no longer a slave but a son, and if a son, then an heir of God through Christ.

Notice here the clear link between adoption and redemption. When we were adopted as sons, Christ paid the price, the ransom, required to set us free from the state of slavery. Thanks to the blood of Jesus, we have two great benefits. First of all we are redeemed from something - slavery to sin. Secondly we are adopted into something - sonship in the Father's love. All this becomes a personal reality when we not only believe by faith that we are adopted but receive by faith the Spirit that so warms our hearts that we look up to heaven and cry, "God Almighty you're my Abba, Father - my Papa and my Dad!" When that happens we "are no longer a slave but a son, and if a son, then an heir of God through Christ."

What a picture!

What a story!

Sons and Soldiers

All this is vital background for our life as freedom fighters. In Paul's day, those adopted into sonship in a Roman family often joined the Roman legions. This was a life of great adventure, travelling the earth, bringing peace and order to a world of warring tribes and barbarian hordes. Then, when they had served their time, they'd use this as a stepping stone into the Senate where they'd enter the governmental sphere, with credibility gained from all their years as soldiers serving under the Emperor's command.

For us this is a helpful picture. We are first and foremost sons of God. Our identity is in our relationship with our Heavenly Father. This relationship of intimacy was won for us at the Cross, through which every person on the planet has access to the Father through Jesus, in the power of the Holy Spirit (Ephesians 2:18). Before anything else therefore we are royal sons by adoption of the Most High God. Our identity is not in our successes but in our sonship. It is in our position not our performance. It is in being not doing.

Secondly, we are soldiers. Having been adopted into sonship, we discover that we haven't signed up for some life of comfort in a leisure club for men. We have signed up to the army of the Lord. In that army we are called each day to wear the armour of God and to take a stand against the wicked schemes that emanate from hell itself. We are called to exercise the power and authority we have in Christ and raise our swords against the darkness, bringing freedom to all those who are as once we were, slaves and orphans, bringing the rule of heaven to earth.

This is foundational to the freedom fighter's cause.

We are first of all sons. That is our royal identity.

We are secondly soldiers. That is our destiny.

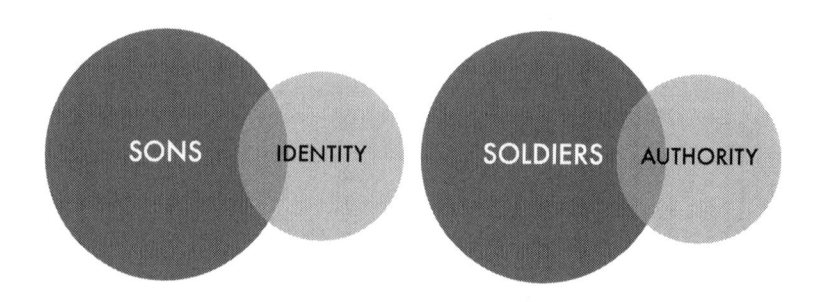

SONS — IDENTITY   SOLDIERS — AUTHORITY

CHAPTER 3 | KNOWING YOUR ENEMY

The Enemy's Master Plan

We shouldn't be under any illusions; when we signed up for the Christian life we didn't find ourselves in a holiday camp; we found ourselves in a boot camp. The authentic Christian life means war. Before you became a follower of Jesus, the enemy did everything to try and prevent you from finding your freedom at the Cross. After you were born again, he has been doing everything he can to try and get you enslaved again. This is the enemy's master plan - to keep those who haven't received Jesus in a perpetual state of slavery and to lure those who have been set free back into the state of bondage from which they have been rescued. To put it succinctly, Jesus is our Strong Deliverer, our Mighty Chain Breaker, and our Loving Liberator. Satan is the exact opposite; he is the one who seeks to keep the sinner in their bondage and seduce the sons of God into the slavery from which they have been redeemed.

This is the master plan of the father of lies; to enslave the world.

This is the master plan of the Father of lights; to liberate the world.

The father of lies is a slave driver.

The Father of lights is a freedom fighter.

What kinds of slavery are we talking about here? What are the chains the enemy uses? There are really two main kinds of slavery that the enemy employs and these are modelled by the two sons in the story of the lavishly loving father in Luke 15.

You know the story: the younger boy gets his dad to hand over his inheritance, goes off to the far country, spends it all on self-indulgent and excessive living, loses everything, realises his folly and then decides to come back home. When he returns, his father welcomes him with open arms and throws a party - enough roast beef for all the villagers. The older brother sees all this and throws a fit. He argues with his father, telling him that he has worked his whole life on the dad's estate and never had a barbeque in his honour. The father's heart is broken as he tells the older son that all he has is his, always has been. The story ends without a resolution. We never get to hear how the boy responds.

These sons in many ways embody the two principal kinds of slavery.

The first, modelled by the younger son, is obvious. This is slavery to sin. We might call it hedonism - the idea that happiness is to be found in seeking to fulfil the pleasures of the flesh through unbridled and excessive living. This almost always leads to an addictive lifestyle in which the person concerned hands over their soul to a power other than God - drugs, food, sex, work, money, for example - and becomes enslaved to the object of their compulsive and fixated focus. The younger son was a son but he chose to become a slave to hedonism.

The older son makes a similar journey without ever leaving home. His problem is not so much hedonism as legalism. He takes the view that he has earned his father's favour through hard work. This is exactly the problem with many of the religious leaders of Jesus' day. They imposed a heavy burden on the people, telling them they needed to gain acceptance from God through works. This too is slavery and the elder brother is a slave. His chains are chains of legalism. He should have lived like a son but he chose to live like a slave.

Let's be clear about this: the enemy is a slave driver and his master plan is to lure people into one of two kinds of slavery: the first is hedonism (the younger son); the second is legalism (the elder son). Both are equally toxic. Both are forms of addiction. Both render people powerless, the first through a compulsive dependency on mood-altering substances and behaviours; the second through an obsessive reliance on mood-altering religious rituals and routines. Both are attachments to things other than the Father's love.

Both are demonic substitutes for the love of all Loves,

Both are forms of bondage.

CHAPTER 3 | KNOWING YOUR ENEMY

Demonic Battle Plans

If this life is a battle, what are freedom fighters to do? The answer is given by the Apostle Paul. In Ephesians 6:11 he tells us to put on the armour of God that we may stand against the wiles, the schemes, and the tactics of the devil. As we have just seen, the enemy's strategy is to enslave us. The Father's main strategy is to set people and indeed the planet free. The question then follows: if the enemy wants to enslave us, what does he use to achieve that goal?

Now it is here that I must issue two vital reminders. The first is that we should understand Paul is speaking to believers in Ephesians 6:10-20. This means that men who follow Jesus can be both attacked and incapacitated by the enemy. Those who say that Christians are immune to demonic assault or enslavement are quite simply wrong. This passage makes it perfectly clear. As Christian men we are to be vigilant. We are to stand guard against the enemy.

The second reminder is this. While we are to understand the enemy's intentions, our focus must never be on the slave driver but on the liberator. Our priority is to worship God - the Father, the Son and the Holy Spirit. It is not to give the enemy any more air time than is absolutely necessary. So while freedom fighters know their enemy's battle plans, their primary passion and priority is to turn on the light not say boo to the darkness.

That said, the Apostle Paul also stated in 2 Corinthians 2:11, "we are not ignorant of his devices." He is referring here to the devices of our enemy. What then are these devices for enslaving us? Let me suggest the following as some of the most obvious ways the enemy uses, both in Scripture and in the freedom fighter's actual experience. You may have encountered some of these assaults yourself:

1. Deception - getting us to believe lies

2. Depravity - getting us to indulge the flesh

3. Division - getting us to fall out with others

4. Doubt - getting us to question what we believe

5. Depression - getting us to feel despondent

6. Dilution - getting us to water down the Gospel

7. Distraction - getting us to focus on problems

Through these and other means the enemy seeks to enslave the adopted sons of God. His perverse longing is to destabilise us so that we forget who we are in Christ (our identity as sons) and what we have in Christ (our authority as soldiers). When his demonic battle plans succeed, Christian men are taken out. They find themselves enslaved to ways of thinking, speaking and acting that are contrary to who they truly are in Christ. They find themselves in bondage, no longer able to set others free because they themselves aren't free.

How will we ever be able to stand against such destructive, demonic tactics?

The Father's Armour

The answer is provided by the Apostle Paul in Ephesians 6:10-20. We are more than able to stand against these wicked and insidious devices of the enemy. For every one of the methods of attack mentioned above, the Father has an answer. Every piece of His armour is designed to match and master these assaults.

Let's look at each piece very briefly.

The belt of **truth** is our sure defence against the tactic of **deception**. When we daily walk in the truth of the Word of God, we know for sure what's true in the sight of God, and what's false too. We are therefore able to recognise error for what it is and stand upon the truth provided by God's Word, especially if we have each other's backs as men.

The breastplate of **righteousness** is our sure defence against the tactic of **depravity**. When we daily walk in the truth of the Word of God, we know what's right in the sight of God and what's wrong

CHAPTER 3 | KNOWING YOUR ENEMY

too. When our hearts are protected by God's Word, the tactic of depravity can be warded off, especially if we have each other's backs as men.

The shoes of the Gospel of **peace** are our sure defence against the tactic of **division**. When we daily walk in the truth of the Word of God, we know what unites us and what divides us. We are therefore able to recognise divisive beliefs and behaviour for what they are and stand upon the truth provided by God's Word, especially if we have each other's backs as men.

The shield of **faith** is our sure defence against the tactic of **doubt**. When we daily walk in the truth of the Word of God, our faith in the goodness and greatness of God grows and grows. We are therefore able to recognise doubts for what they are and stand upon the truth provided by God's Word, especially if we have each other's backs as men.

The helmet of **salvation** is our sure defence against the tactic of **depression**. When we daily fill our minds with the truth of the Word of God, we know for sure that our history is healed, our identity sealed and our destiny revealed. We are therefore able to recognise demonic, mental strongholds and cast them down, especially if we have each other's backs as men.

The sword of the Spirit, **the Word of God,** is our sure defence against the tactic of **dilution**. When we daily walk in God's Word, we keep our thinking in alignment with the mind of Christ rather than with the thinking of this world, thereby ensuring that the tactic of diluting the Gospel can be warded off, especially if we have each other's backs as men.

The practice of **praying in the Spirit** is our sure defence against the tactic of **distraction**. When we daily pray in the Spirit, we allow our minds to focus on what Jesus wants us to pray about rather on the problems the enemy uses to distract us. We are therefore able to keep our hearts on kingdom priorities, especially if we have each other's backs as men.

Do you see how our Heavenly Father has given us the equipment we need to guard our freedom? Every piece of His armour is meticulously designed in heaven to protect the adopted sons of God as they war against the enemy here on the earth. Every part of the soldier's kit is tailor-made to combat and conquer the demonic battle plans of the enemy, from deception to distraction and everything between. We have more than we need to be conquerors.

We have truth around our waists.

We have righteousness covering our hearts.

We have peace as our footwear.

We have faith as our shield.

We have salvation covering our minds.

We have the Word of God as our sword.

And we have prayer as our focus.

With these weapons of war we can be effective in staying free ourselves and bringing freedom to the lives of those whom the Father wants us to serve.

Freedom fighters are healing warriors. We set the captives free and we bring healing to a planet longing for the revelation of the sons of God.

We were once orphans but now we are the adopted children of God.

We were once bound but now we have been redeemed.

We once were slaves but now we are sons.

Now we are free people, setting others free!

CHAPTER 3 | KNOWING YOUR ENEMY

APPLYING THE FREEDOM FIGHTING PRINCIPLES

What am I going to *do* in response to what I've read in this chapter?

Action Point 1

_____

Action Point 2

_____

Action Point 3

_____

What am I going to pray for as a result of what I've read?

Prayer Point 1

_____

Prayer Point 2

_____

Prayer Point 3

_____

PERSONAL TRAINING:

Spend some time considering the questions in the box and bring these to the Lord in prayer.

WHICH OF THESE ENEMY TACTICS HAVE BEEN USED AGAINST ME PERSONALLY?

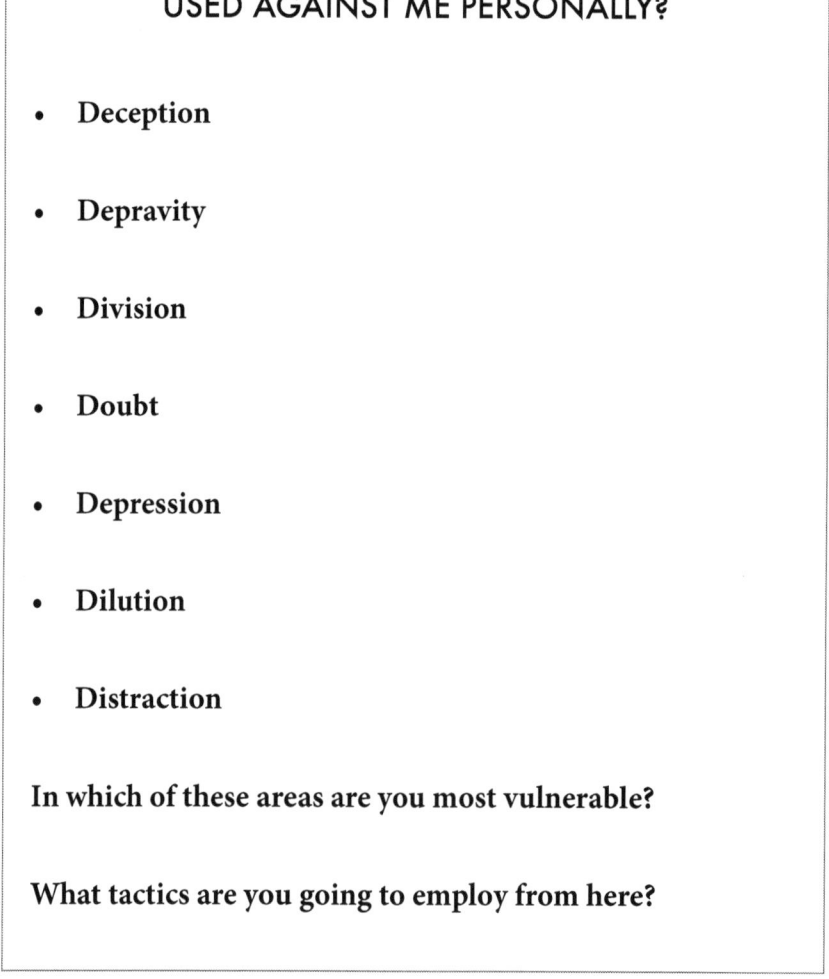

- **Deception**

- **Depravity**

- **Division**

- **Doubt**

- **Depression**

- **Dilution**

- **Distraction**

In which of these areas are you most vulnerable?

What tactics are you going to employ from here?

CHAPTER 3 | KNOWING YOUR ENEMY

GROUP TRAINING:

WHICH OF THESE ENEMY TACTICS HAVE BEEN USED AGAINST YOU AS MEN?

- Deception

- Depravity

- Division

- Doubt

- Depression

- Dilution

- Distraction

How are you going to help those who have become enslaved?

How are you going to guard against future enemy attacks?

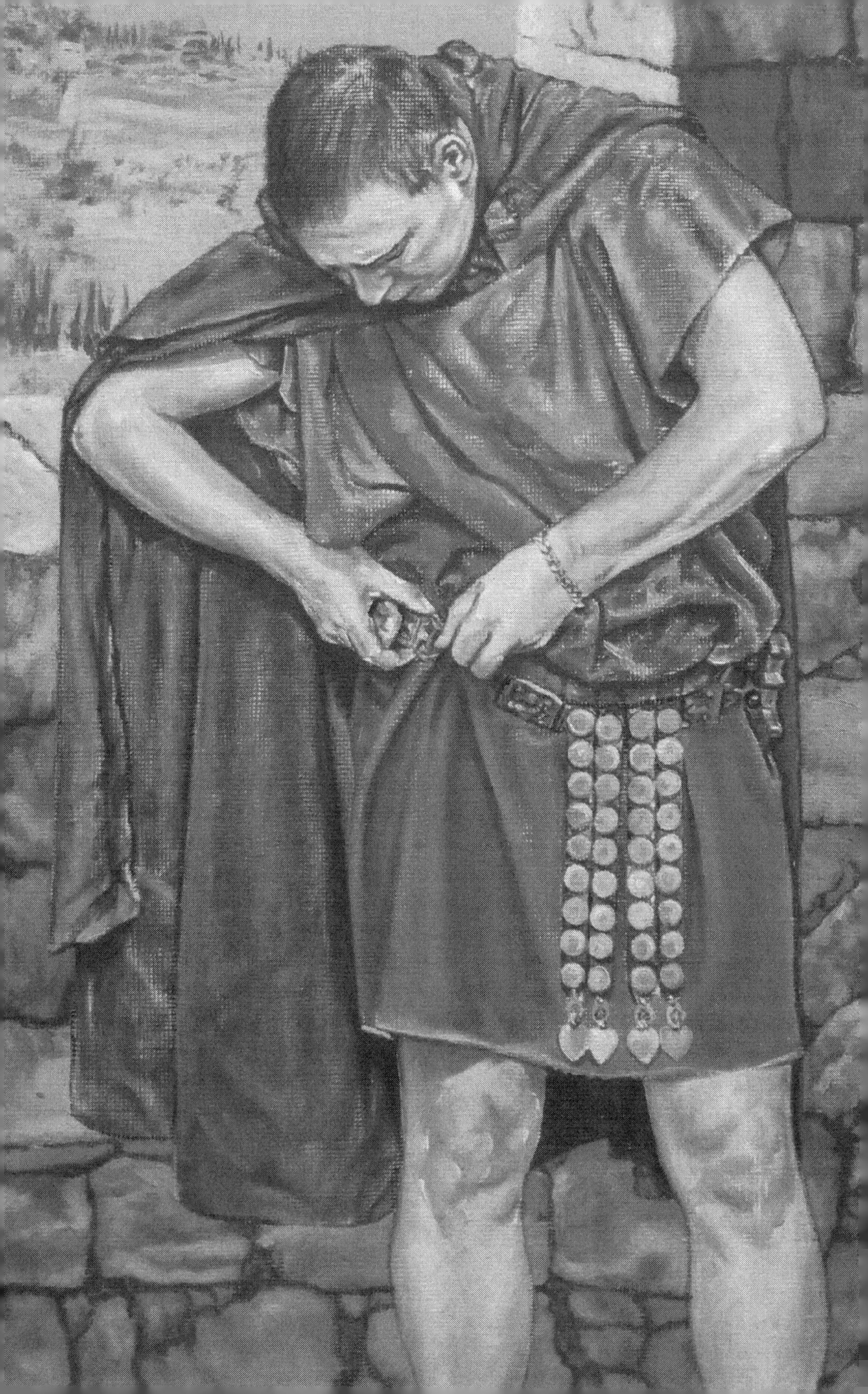

CHAPTER 4

WEARING YOUR BELT

Imagine for a moment that you are a young Jewish boy, say nine years old, running on the streets of Jerusalem around AD 30. You are playing with several other friends, laughing as you chase each other through the crowded alleyways and the bustling markets. Suddenly you and your friends stop still. You can hear the sound of jangling metal and crunching boots. You dash into the entrance of a shop and stare out towards the sound. As you do, you see scores of Roman legionaries marching in perfect ranks down the centre of the main street. They are led by a centurion with a gloriously plumed helmet seated on a caparisoned horse. For a moment, the spectacle takes your breath away.

The local traders and buyers part like the Red Sea in front of the officer and his troops. You watch, wide eyed and open mouthed, as the legionaries march by, their bronze body armour clinking against their metal belt buckles, the nail studs on the soles of their feet marking out a perfect rhythm on the stone streets, their eyes fixed in a look of extreme concentration on the centurion in front of them.

Even though they are pagans, carrying the insignia of Caesar, you cannot help being overwhelmed by the impressive sights and sounds of these marching men.

Later you will fashion a small sword and a shield out of wood from your father's carpentry shop and play at being warring soldiers with your friends.

However much you hate them, you will never forget them.

Their armour will gleam in the darkest recesses of your memory for the rest of your life.

The distant bark of the officer's commands will often wake you in the middle of the night.

The First Piece of Armour

When the Apostle Paul thought about how to finish his letter to the Ephesians he was now a prisoner of Rome. He was in chains in a damp and cold jail cell, guarded by Roman soldiers. As he considered how he was to compose his final exhortation, the Holy Spirit drew his attention to the men either side of him in their splendid armour.

'I know how to conclude this letter,' Paul mused. 'I'll issue a call to arms and encourage my congregations to stand firm like spiritual legionaries.'

As that idea began to inspire him, he reflected on the armour pieces and began to see each item of the soldier's panoply as symbols. The first of the items he mentions is the belt and he refers to this as the belt of truth.

Stand therefore, having girded your waist with truth.

[Ephesians 6.14]

In the original text, Paul doesn't actually mention a belt. However, he does use the Greek verb *perizonnumi*, which means 'to fasten a belt', and the noun *osphus* which means 'the hips' or 'waist,' so we can be sure that the Apostle has in mind the belt to which the Roman soldier's sword and dagger were attached.

To get a true picture we need to remember that the first item a Roman soldier would have put on in the morning was a white, short-sleeved tunic that extended to his knees. This was kept in place over his body not only by his breastplate but more importantly by his

CHAPTER 4 | WEARING YOUR BELT

belt, which held everything together at the very centre of his body.

The belt worn by the Roman legionary in Paul's era was known in Latin as the *balteus* and was one of the main things that distinguished a soldier from a civilian. Usually this took the form of a single waist belt made with leather and decorated with embossed bronze plates. These belt plates were given intricate designs made out of niello, a black alloy of silver and sulphur. When a man wore a belt like this it was a sure sign that he was a soldier which is why the Roman poet Juvenal referred to the legionaries as 'armed and belted men.'

The belt was not just a practical piece of equipment. It was also a symbol of a man's identity as a soldier. Just as in today's world a detective is divested of their identity when their police badge is taken from them, so in the Roman world of Paul's day a soldier was deprived of their identity when their belt was removed. If a soldier was dishonourably discharged, their belt was taken away. If insurgents wanted to disorient soldiers in a crowd, they used daggers to slice the belts from their hips.

Don't therefore underestimate the significance of the belt! Just because it seems relatively unimpressive compared to the other pieces doesn't mean for a moment that it is trivial. The legionary's *balteus* was quite literally central to him; it held everything in place.

Believing and Behaving

Before we look in detail at what the belt represents, I need to make some general comments about each of the pieces of armour in Ephesians 6.

There has long been a debate among Bible scholars about whether each of these pieces refers to something doctrinal or something ethical. Put more simply, scholars have asked the following question: do these pieces of armour represent things that we are called to believe or ways in which we are meant to behave?

If we take the first item of armour, we can see why people ask this question. Truth can mean one of two things here:

1) The Truth about Jesus

If the belt refers to that, then Paul is saying, "Make sure, brothers, you always keep the truth about Jesus central to your lives."

2) The Truth in General

If the belt refers to that, then Paul is saying, "Make sure, brothers, the practice of telling the truth is always a central and core value in your life."

You can see how Paul's economy with words leads to such divergent opinions. Paul chooses not to tell us which of these he has in mind. In my view, there can only be one reason:

Paul means both!

Since the time of Jesus, Christians have fought hard to hold the line in two great and important fields of battle: the first is right beliefs and the second is right behaviour. The first is often referred to as "Orthodoxy". The second is referred to as "Orthopraxy". Many Christians have lived and died to defend "right teaching" and "right actions".

If men want to be freedom fighters, they need to fight for right beliefs and right behaviour. They need to be constantly on guard against one of the enemy's chief tactics which is deception. As we saw briefly in the last chapter, the enemy wants to disable God's legionaries on earth. One of his malevolent battle plans is to use deception. He wants to get Christian men to lose their confidence in the truth of God's Word and even to question it. He wants us to stop being truthful about ourselves and others and to start believing his lies.

Paul therefore had both belief and behaviour in mind with each item of the armour. As a spiritual father, he urged Timothy to guard both: "Keep a close watch on how you live and on your teaching.

CHAPTER 4 | WEARING YOUR BELT

Stay true to what is right for the sake of your own salvation and the salvation of those who hear you" (1 Timothy 4:16). In the Message, Eugene Peterson renders the verse as follows: "Keep a firm grasp on both your character and your teaching. Don't be diverted. Just keep at it. Both you and those who hear you will experience salvation."

As we look at each of the pieces of armour in the coming chapters, we will look at what each has to see about both the freedom fighter's beliefs and the freedom fighter's behaviour.

The Reason Why

When Jesus appeared before Pontius Pilate, the Roman governor asked him, "What is truth?" This is a question that can only have one answer as far as the freedom fighter is concerned. For us, the truth is not a philosophy, it is a person. That person is Jesus, who described Himself as "the Way, the Truth and the Life" (John 14:6). Pilate's question is therefore deeply ironic. In asking the question, the answer is quite literally staring at him in the face!

Jesus provides the true truth about everything in the cosmos. That is a big claim, I know, but remember what John told us in the grand opening of his Gospel: "In the beginning was the Word" (John 1:1). He is talking about Jesus here. Jesus is God's Word, God's Final Word indeed. The prophets had spoken the word of God over many centuries. This had given God's people a progressive revelation of the truth. Now, with the advent of Jesus, God has spoken His final, exhaustive, complete revelation to human beings. This is why in Hebrews 1:1-2 we read, "God, who at various times and in various ways spoke in time past to the fathers by the prophets, has in these last days spoken to us by *His* Son."

It is really fascinating to dwell for a moment on the word "Word" in John 1. What did John mean? There have been so many interpretations over the centuries but my view is that John was writing his Gospel in Ephesus and that the answer lies in the history of that city - in John's day located in Asia Minor, what we today refer to as Turkey.

Five hundred years or so before John was born there was a philosopher who lived in Ephesus. His name was Heraclitus. He lived a fairly solitary life and was known for being rather melancholy. Indeed, he was nicknamed "the weeping philosopher." I suppose he was to philosophy what Jeremiah was to prophecy.

Renowned for his obscure sayings, Heraclitus started talking to his students about a mysterious reality called the logos. This is the word that John uses when he says five centuries later, "In the beginning was the Word." In Heraclitus' mind, it meant "the reason why." His passion in life was to find out the reason why everything behaved in the way it did.

It was with this in mind that the tearful philosopher would set his students an ongoing challenge: "Find out the reason why the weather behaves in the way it does, why the stars behave in the way they do, why human beings behave in the way they do, why the mind behaves in the way it does, why the gods behave in the way they do."

Even to this day, Heraclitus' influence can be felt in our language. In all the examples I just mentioned, we can see his legacy in the following nouns:

Meteorology - how the weather behaves

Astrology - how the stars behave

Anthropology - how human beings behave

Theology - how God behaves.

Notice how the word logos is at the end of each! When students set themselves to understanding these things, they continue Heraclitus' quest to find the reason why.

And then John - a simple fisherman - starts putting pen to paper, sometime between about 50 and 90 AD. As he starts writing his Gospel, the Holy Spirit starts to whisper to him:

"Do you remember how that great philosopher in your city was always going on about the logos - the reason why?"

"Yes, yes, I do."

"Well I'm going to let you in on a secret."

"What's that?"

"Jesus is the Reason Why."

"What do you mean?"

"Jesus is the answer to every question. He is Ultimate Meaning and True Truth. Everything human beings long to have answered is in Him. Everything is answered not by a philosophy but by a person - the One and Only son of God!"

With that, John reached out with his quill, dipped it in some ink, and scratched the following words on a papyrus scroll: "The Word became flesh and dwelt among us, and we beheld His glory, the glory as of the only begotten of the Father, full of grace and truth" (John 1:14).

Imagine that.

The Reason Why became a human being.

The answer to everything was revealed - in a baby lying and crying in a manger!

Fighting for the Truth

At this point you may well be feeling the pull of the world's way of thinking. You see, the world doesn't think like this. In contemporary culture, people's thinking has been radically affected and influenced by two philosophies. These are:

1. Pluralism - the view that there is no one place where you find truth but a plurality of places.

2. Relativism - the view that nothing is absolutely true but everything is relatively true.

These two philosophies are so embedded in our educational systems, and indeed our mass media, that even freedom fighters may be tempted to say something like this:

"You can't say that Jesus is true Truth. People today believe that he's one truth among many, and that every truth claim must be given an equal voice."

While there is a positive sides to these philosophies (not least their basis in respecting other people's views), there is also a negative side. These ideas have a strong hold over the minds of countless people, especially in the Western World. In particular, they affect the way a Christian man speaks about Jesus. Instead of saying, "I respect your right to say what you believe, but my conviction is that Jesus is the Truth, not just a truth," we are tempted to say, "Jesus was truthful, but so were other great religious leaders."

Freedom fighters cannot surrender to such compromises.

Just as the Roman legionary was unwavering in his belief about the supremacy of Caesar, so the freedom fighter is unflinching in his conviction about the supremacy of Christ.

Notice I said "conviction".

As someone once said, a belief is something you hold. A conviction is something that holds you.

Freedom fighters are held by the belief that Jesus is Lord, that Jesus is the Truth, that Jesus is the Only Saviour, that Jesus is the One and Only Son of the Living God.

Freedom fighters place this truth that is Jesus at the centre of their lives, like a Roman soldier's belt around his waist. Christian men contend for the truth. They fight for the Christian worldview, as revealed in the Bible. They are defenders of the faith which is faith in Jesus Christ. They do not tolerate any hint of heresy in the

CHAPTER 4 | WEARING YOUR BELT

church and they confront in love the wrong thinking in the world.

Demolishing Strongholds

One of the things a Roman legionary would almost certainly have to do during his service was storm a citadel. These citadels were situated on the top of high hills or mountains. They looked over entire landscapes, providing a fortified vantage point for controlling whole regions. These strongholds had to be taken if the Roman army was going to occupy a territory. Capture the citadel and you conquered the country.

The Apostle Paul had this in mind when he addressed the Christian congregation he had planted in the city of Corinth: "The weapons of our warfare are not carnal but mighty in God for pulling down strongholds, casting down arguments and every high thing that exalts itself against the knowledge of God, bringing every thought into captivity to the obedience of Christ" (2 Corinthians 10:4-5).

Notice three things here about "strongholds".

First of all, notice the **nature** of these strongholds. Paul uses the idea of a stronghold to describe how the enemy works. Just as a physical stronghold is situated in a high place and controls an entire area, so a spiritual stronghold is situated in a high place and controls an entire area. In the case of a spiritual stronghold, it is the human mind that functions as the citadel. The mind, associated at least in part with the brain, is at the highest place in a person's body. Once the mind is captured by the enemy, then an entire area is captured too - in other words, the whole of a person's life. What a person believes affects how a person behaves. Believe wrong things and you'll behave in the wrong way. When the enemy has a strong hold over people's thinking, it's not long before they start behaving in wrong ways - in ways that are destructive for human health and relationships.

Secondly, notice what Paul says about the **purpose** of these strongholds. Yes they are designed to hold the mind captive to wrong thinking. But why does the enemy do this? It is so that a person will not think the right way about God. He will believe human arguments that obstruct him in his ability to know God in an intimate, personal and relational way. Jesus came to reconcile us with our perfect, Heavenly Father. The enemy is determined that our minds will not accept this truth. So he fills our thinking with pluralism (the lie that says, "There are many ways to God, not just Jesus") and relativism (the lie that says, "Nothing is absolutely true; everything is relatively true"). These philosophies have a demonic origin and a demonic purpose. They are born out of "lying spirits" or out of "the spirit of deception." The enemy uses these spirits to stop us knowing who God really is and who we really are:

That God is Abba, Father - the best, most affirming and affectionate Dad in the universe...

That we are the adopted sons and daughters of God, for whom the universe has been waiting!

Notice finally what Paul says about the **defeat** of these strongholds. Freedom fighters can take captive the very spirits that have taken people captive! They can demolish the strong holds that the enemy has had over the high places in people's lives - their minds! With the help of the power of the Holy Spirit, these citadels and fortresses of the mind can be utterly demolished so that a person's thoughts can be taken captive to Christ rather than Satan. In other words, a person can change their minds and have their thinking submitted to the truth of heaven rather than the lies of hell. They can learn to think like Jesus and every area of their lives can be brought under the reign of heaven, the Kingdom of God.

And this is true freedom.

True freedom isn't found in thinking any way you like, or in thinking the same thoughts as people who belong to an intellectually corrupt culture.

True freedom is found in thinking the way Jesus thinks. When that happens, you know the truth and the truth sets you and others free.

The One Fixed Point

Heraclitus was a man obsessed by the fact that everything seemed to change and nothing seemed to remain constant. Perhaps this was why he became "the weeping philosopher". He saw that the essence of the universe was its constantly changing nature. Everything was in flux. Nothing seemed to be fixed. So, with his typical melancholy, he came up with an obscure saying: "No man ever steps in the same river twice." No wonder, according to Diogenes, he ended up wandering the mountains alone, living on a diet of grass and herbs. After smearing himself with dung, it is said that Heraclitus was devoured by dogs.

Do you see the end result of harmful strongholds over people's thinking? Heraclitus couldn't get his bearings. For all his searching, he couldn't find the ultimate reason why in the universe. He believed that "everything flows." Nothing is fixed. "All entities move," he declared, "and nothing remains still." Everything is in a state of becoming and finds itself somewhere between waxing and waning.

Can you see how destructive beliefs lead to self-destructive behaviour?

Richard Rorty was an American philosopher who died in 2007. Rorty's mind was held captive to the stronghold of relativism. He allowed his thinking to be moulded by the lie that nothing is absolutely true but everything is relatively true. This is obviously self-contradictory! As many have pointed out, in claiming that there are no absolute truths, Rorty and others have uttered what they regard as an absolute truth! This just goes to show that the devil specialises in nonsense - in non-sense that masquerades as sense. In denying that there is objective truth, Rorty has said something that sounds objectively true!

On one famous occasion Rorty is said to have argued that truth is what everyone in a room agrees is true. In other words, truth is not defined by God but by communities of people. But what if everyone in the room is deceived? What about Hitler's generals at Eagle's Nest, perched at the top of an Austrian mountain? When they all agreed that the Jewish people should be subjected to their "final solution", was this true too? The answer is plain to anyone with common sense. It was a destructive deception, born out of their immersion in an occult world that led their thinking into the deepest darkness.

Rorty believed that there is no timeless, objective or absolute truth but that we all adopt what he called "contingent vocabularies", which is a rather pretentious way of saying that we accept particular ways of talking about what works and doesn't work, depending on where we live and what era we happen to be living in. Rorty once famously said, "The truth cannot be out there!" To him, nothing was sacred. Everything was subject to change. The most basic assumptions of philosophy can be deconstructed. Truth is something people agree about at any given time. It is not "out there". It is what groups of people agree is pragmatic - what works!

Rorty's writings have been extremely influential. In the hugely successful stage musical called Wicked, the Wizard tells the boy Alfie, "The truth is not fact or reason. The truth is just what everyone agrees on!" That's Rorty right there! Freedom fighters should not let this kind of thing go, especially if they are dads whose children are listening to this kind of thing.

Freedom fighters contend for true truth.

They don't deny that the world is constantly changing.

But they affirm that Jesus Christ is the one fixed point in a changing universe.

Telling the Truth

Freedom fighters therefore put on the belt of truth. Every day, they make sure that true truth is at the centre of their lives. If Jesus is the one fixed point in a changing universe, if he is the Reason Why in every sphere of life, then the Christian legionary will place this belief at the very centre of their lives. Since truth is a person not a philosophy, what this really means is that freedom fighters keep the person of Jesus at the centre of their lives. Everything they believe about Jesus must be consistent with what the Bible teaches. Everything they believe about the world must be consistent with what Jesus teaches. For the freedom fighter, wearing the belt of truth means singing, "Jesus, be the centre."

Furthermore, wearing the belt of truth applies to behaviour. What we believe deeply affects how we behave - a point made by the critics of Richard Rorty, who accused him of leading countless young people into a cynicism about right and wrong that in turn led to self-destructive behaviour. For the freedom fighter, it is not enough to believe that Jesus is true truth. They will want also to be truthful. They will want to have a true view of themselves and of others and they will want to speak the truth in love rather than lie or tell half truths.

For the freedom fighter, integrity is everything. If a man believes that Jesus is the Truth, then he will want to not only defend this in the public space but live it out in the private sphere by being a man who can be trusted always to tell the truth. He will not believe lies about himself or others. He will not bear false witness about another person or gossip about them. He will be a truth-teller in private as well as in public. He will hold fast to the value of truthfulness, making that a central value in his daily life.

So you see how the belt of truth is a matter of both believing the right things and behaving in the right way. This should not surprise us. It has long been noticed that belief and behaviour cannot be separated in Paul's mind. The first three chapters of Ephesians are very much about right believing. They are doctrinal in content. The second three chapters are very much about right behaving. They are ethical in content. In Paul's thinking, right believing and right behaving are inextricably connected. Once you believe correctly you can behave correctly; your creed will always influence and determine your conduct. That is why, in the same letter that he describes the armour of God, Paul says,

"Therefore, putting away lying. Let each one of you speak truth with his neighbour, for we are members of one another" [Ephesians 4:25]

In conclusion, the freedom fighter is committed to truth. This means that the Christian man is not a relativist – he is not someone who regards every worldview as relatively true, including the Christian one. No, the Christian man today puts the belt of truth around his waist. He dresses himself with Biblical, Christian truth every day. He immerses himself in God's timeless Word which contains eternal and absolute truth and he makes this true truth central to everything in his life, like a belt that holds everything together.

At the same time, the Christian man is a man who not only believes the truth; he behaves in a truthful way. He is known for his consistency. He commends the truth of what he believes by behaving with such integrity that he develops a reputation for always being a truth-teller. In this way his truthfulness as a man points people to the truthfulness of his message - that Jesus is the Way, the Truth and the Life. He is a freedom fighter who not only guards the truth of the Gospel but also the importance of being a truthful and therefore trustworthy man.

So don't forget to put on your belt!

Freedom fighters get free and stay free.

They demolish the enemy's strongholds in their own lives and then they join with other freedom fighters to demolish the enemy's strongholds in their culture.

CHAPTER 4 | WEARING YOUR BELT

APPLYING THE FREEDOM FIGHTING PRINCIPLES

What am I going to *do* in response to what I've read in this chapter?

Action Point 1

_____

Action Point 2

_____

Action Point 3

_____

What am I going to pray for as a result of what I've read?

Prayer Point 1

_____

Prayer Point 2

_____

Prayer Point 3

_____

PERSONAL TRAINING:

Spend some time considering the questions in the box and bring these to the Lord in prayer.

> To what extent have you been a champion and guardian of true truth?
>
> Do you find it easy to defend true truth (Jesus) when you're with those who are held captive by relativism?
>
> What can you do to bring freedom to those who have wrong beliefs?
>
> What can you do personally to keep your mind free from deception?
>
> In what ways can you cultivate a lifestyle of truth-telling?
>
> How might you ratchet up your integrity levels?

CHAPTER 4 | WEARING YOUR BELT

GROUP TRAINING:

Are there strongholds over the thinking in your group?

What are you going to do to demolish these wrong ways of thinking?

How can you support one another in being truth-tellers to each other and to those with whom you interact?

Are there people you know who are bound by deception and to whom you need to bring freedom?

Why not engage now in a corporate act in which you put on the belt of truth and make a commitment to being truthful in what you believe and how you behave?

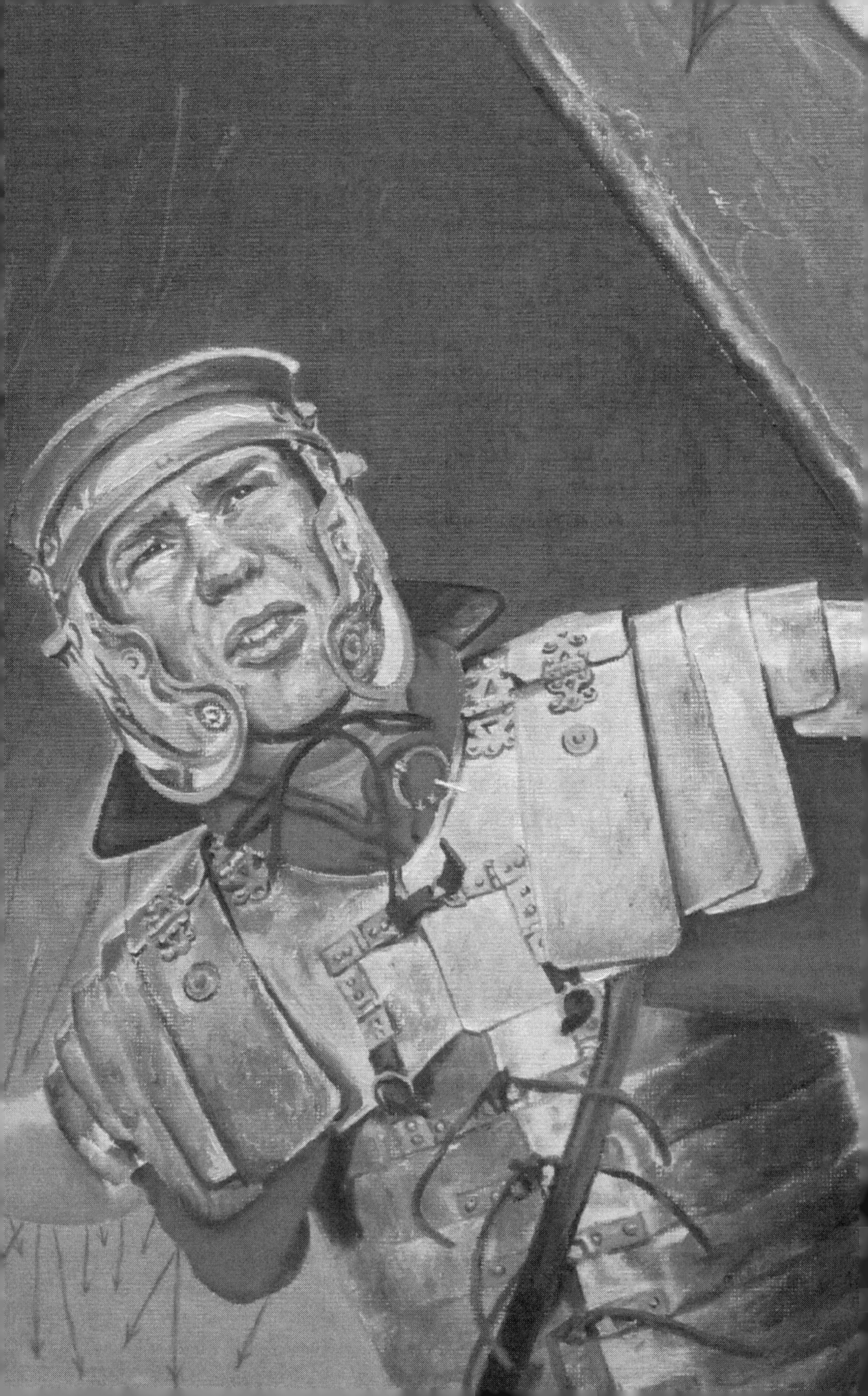

CHAPTER 5

GUARDING YOUR HEART

When you imagine a Roman legionary, what do you see? I'm sure you see him with his plumed helmet and a raised shield but I'm also fairly certain that his breastplate will spring to mind. The breastplate was one of the most important items in the Roman soldier's armour. As the ancient historian Polybius wrote, "The common soldiers wear a breastplate of brass a span square, which they place in front of the heart and call the heart-protector *(pectorale)*."

Roman soldiers in the New Testament era usually fought wearing heavy chest plates. Some were equipped with very light armour. They were called *expeditii* and advanced in front of the legionaries with pila or light missiles, fighting skirmishes before the main body of troops crashed into the front ranks of their enemies. But most legionaries wore a breastplate - an articulated piece of armour made up of iron hoops and plates and edged with bronze.

This breastplate weighed about 20lbs and was worn over a padded garment that prevented the armour from grazing the skin, absorbed the blows when the armour was struck, and held the armour tightly in place. This breastplate protected the soldier's back, shoulders, chest and stomach. In particular, it afforded a robust covering for the legionary's heart.

As Polybius put it, the soldier's breastplate was his *pectorale*, his 'heart protector' and no freedom fighter can afford to neglect it.

Just as If I'd Never Sinned

As the Apostle Paul continues his description of each piece of our spiritual armour, he tells his readers to stand "having put on the breastplate of righteousness." Now keep in mind what I wrote earlier about each piece of armour representing both belief and behaviour. As Paul mentored his spiritual son Timothy, he counselled him to keep a close and careful eye on both what he believed (doctrine) and how he behaved (lifestyle). In the case of the belt of truth, we saw how this applied. Paul encourages us to put truth at the centre of our lives. Truth refers to both belief and behaviour. Jesus Christ, as the Word of God, is true Truth. The Bible, as the Word of God, is true Truth. Wearing the belt means keeping God's Word central to all our beliefs. It also means being truthful; in other words, making integrity a central and core value in our lives and a primary quality in our daily behaviour.

When we come to righteousness, we need to bear this twofold application in mind. This means that when we think of righteousness, we must first of all think of wearing over our hearts something that is crucial to our beliefs as Christian men in the 21st century. What then did Paul have in mind?

When Paul used the word righteousness he was thinking at least in part of a law court scenario. Righteousness is one of the greatest attributes of God. He is always in the right. He knows right from wrong and His definition of what constitutes good and evil behaviour is absolute and eternal not relative and temporal. Originally, human beings were righteous. Adam and Eve did what was right in the sight of God - until, that is, they ate the forbidden fruit of the Tree of Knowledge. This choice proved catastrophic not just for them but for the whole of the human race thereafter. From that moment on every human being became by nature unrighteous. In other words, as a direct result of our first parent's sin, every one of us is innately sinful, preferring to live a self-centred rather than a God-centred life, thereby leaning always

CHAPTER 5 | GUARDING YOUR HEART

towards doing what is wrong rather than what is right.

Human beings could not rectify this problem. All the good works and fine rituals in the world could not make us "in the right" again. But God, not wishing us to go on paying the price for Adam's sin, sent His One and Only Son into the world to put things right. Jesus Christ born in Bethlehem and grew up to be a man. During His life, He was tempted in every way as we are and yet he never sinned; he never gave way to saying or doing the wrong thing. On the Cross, this perfect Saviour took all our unrighteousness, all our sinfulness, in His body. He became unrighteous for our sakes. He who was never in the wrong became someone in the wrong so that we who are in the wrong could be declared by God to be in the right. That, by any accounts, is a glorious exchange. We who deserved nothing but death received Christ's righteousness and Christ, who did not deserve death at all, received our unrighteousness.

This is the majesty of Calvary. Two thousand years ago, Jesus died on the Cross so that we, who could not help or rescue ourselves, could be declared righteous by God. This startling truth is Good News, which is why it is known as the Gospel. Thanks to Christ's sacrifice, we are "justified" - we can say of ourselves, through no merit of our own, "It is just-as-if-I'd never sinned!" That really is something worth believing!

And that's what putting on the breastplate means. It means every day and every night believing in our hearts that we have been justified before God not through our religious works but through the shedding of Christ's blood.

This is truly our heart protector. God, the perfect judge, has declared us "not guilty" in heaven.

This has not happened through our good deeds.

It is the result of the finished work of the Cross.

The ABC of Righteousness

If you and I want to be freedom fighters, then we need to believe the right things. We need to believe what I call the ABC about righteousness.

A means **ADMITTING** that every human being is by nature unrighteous. In other words, we need to admit, and get others to admit, that we are incapable of living a righteous life on our own terms and in our own strength. Every attempt to leave God out of the picture leads to getting it wrong. All of us are therefore sinners. As Paul says in Romans 3:11-15 (The Message):

> *There's nobody living right, not even one,*
>   *nobody who knows the score, nobody alert for God.*
> *They've all taken the wrong turn;*
>   *they've all wandered down blind alleys.*
> *No one's living right;*
>   *I can't find a single one.*
> *Their throats are gaping graves,*
>   *their tongues slick as mudslides.*
> *Every word they speak is tinged with poison.*
>   *They open their mouths and pollute the air.*
> *They race for the honour of sinner-of-the-year,*
>   *litter the land with heartbreak and ruin,*
> *Don't know the first thing about living with others.*
>   *They never give God the time of day.*

The first step is therefore to admit that everyone is in the wrong in the sight of a righteous God - that we are all sinners and that we all fall well short of God's holy, perfect and righteous standards.

The second step is to **BELIEVE** that Jesus Christ, the Righteous One, did what we could not do for ourselves; He lived a life of perfect righteousness and His righteousness is the gift that He freely gives to us. As Paul puts it in Romans 3:23-24 (The Message):

> *Since we've compiled this long and sorry record as sinners (both*

CHAPTER 5 | GUARDING YOUR HEART

us and them) and proved that we are utterly incapable of living the glorious lives God wills for us, God did it for us. Out of sheer generosity he put us in right standing with himself. A pure gift. He got us out of the mess we're in and restored us to where he always wanted us to be. And he did it by means of Jesus Christ.

If the second step is to believe that Christ has given us right standing before God, the third is to **COMMIT** ourselves every day to wearing the righteousness of Christ. Our own righteousness is no righteousness at all. But when we repent of our sins and believe that Jesus paid the price at Calvary, we receive the righteousness of Christ. It is this that enables us to proceed to step three which is to COMMIT to living every day of our lives in right standing before God. We do this by wearing Christ's righteousness and living as Christ lived while He was a man here on the earth. As Paul puts it in Romans 3:25-26 (The Message):

God sacrificed Jesus on the altar of the world to clear that world of sin. Having faith in him sets us in the clear. God decided on this course of action in full view of the public—to set the world in the clear with himself through the sacrifice of Jesus, finally taking care of the sins he had so patiently endured. This is not only clear, but it's now—this is current history! God sets things right. He also makes it possible for us to live in his rightness.

So here's the ABC of righteousness:

A = Admit that every one of us is in the wrong and that we can't rescue ourselves

B = Believe that Christ did what we couldn't do and rectified our wrongs at Calvary

C = Commit to a life of wearing Christ's righteousness and remaining "in the right"

Walking the Right Way

This third step begs the question, "what does it mean to remain in the right?" The answer is simple: it means to keep doing the right things. What are the right things? The Bible has the answer. Doing the right thing means to keep behaving as Jesus behaved. This means asking every time we have an ethical decision or dilemma, "What would Jesus do?" When we look carefully at the choices that Jesus made in the Gospels we have everything we need to help us know what the right thing is. Sometimes this may need to be weighed with other, mature Christian brothers, but what is right will always become clear as together we seek to make Christ-centred, Biblically-based and Spirit-led choices. This what mature sons do; they find out what pleases their Father and they do it, without hesitation!

Righteousness therefore has a moral meaning. It refers to our behaviour not just to our beliefs. Remaining "in the right" means continuing to walk in the way Jesus walked while He was on earth as a human being. For this reason, Paul deals in Ephesians (the same letter where he describes the armour of God) with imitating the Father as his dear children. He calls us to live as sons and daughters whose thoughts, words and actions reflect the counter-cultural values of heaven. He tells us how we should speak (5.2-4), how we should express our sexuality (5.5), how we should manage our time (5.15-16), how we should control our drinking habits (5.18-21), how we should conduct our marital relationships (5.22-33), how we should maintain harmony in the home (6.1-4) and how we should conduct ourselves in the workplace (5-9).

This is Paul's practical holiness code for daily life. Paul wants us to know that we have to wear Christ's righteousness over our hearts. That is the believing side of the equation. But he also wants us to say and do the right things, according to the standards of God's absolute and eternally binding understanding right and wrong. That is the behaving side of the equation. The true soldier of Christ, the true freedom fighter, keeps his heart free from everything that would undermine this belief that by faith we are made righteous in the sight of God. Likewise, he keeps his heart free from anything

CHAPTER 5 | GUARDING YOUR HEART

and everything that would lead him away from saying and doing the right thing in God's eyes.

This is what it means to wear the breastplate of righteousness; it means to keep our hearts focused on believing the right things and behaving in the right ways.

When Great Men Fall

David was a remarkable leader and yet he fell spectacularly. He fell because he allowed his strength to become his weakness. One of his strengths was the ability to create strategies that would bring victory in battle. When he saw and lusted after Bathsheba one day, he used this same strategic ability to fulfil his desires. He made plans to commit adultery with Bathsheba and to put her husband in a situation of certain death. He then used his position as King to orchestrate the fulfilment of his plans.

The truth eventually came out and David was utterly heart-broken. He began to weep with godly sorrow and deep repentance. He cried out, 'create in me a clean heart, O God, and renew a steadfast spirit within me' (Psalm 51.10). Having experienced moral failure, David implored the Lord that he would create (*bara* in Hebrew, meaning 'to shape, fashion, form') a clean (*tahowr*, morally pure) heart. He prayed for God to do a re-creative miracle.

What was David doing here? If we use the language of Ephesians 6, he was taking up his battered breastplate of righteousness and placing it over his heart once again. The heart is the seat of all our emotions – including feelings of shame, fear, unworthiness and failure. It is the governing centre of all our conduct. As David knew all too well, the heart is the place where all our decisions concerning God are made.

David put the breastplate over his heart again. In his heart, he looked to restore his right standing before God and he resolved to act rightly in his behaviour. In spite of the fact that David had taken another man's wife and effectively killed her husband – a loyal servant of his called Uriah – God heard David's cry. More than that, God saw beyond this very dramatic fall to David's core and later declared what was really true about him. He said that David was a man after his own heart – a man who would do all his will (Acts 13.22). What an extraordinary statement that is! David's failure did not define who he really was. His heart did, and his heart was passionately committed to God's heart, his will to doing God's will.

But some of you may ask, did not David sin greatly? Yes, but God did not allow this huge lapse of judgment to become the final word about David's life. God did not allow this shame to dictate his legacy or determine his destiny.

And here is something even more extraordinary. Jesus Christ, God's Son, would later be born in the line of David. Jesus Christ himself would be called 'Son of David.' If David had been defined by failure, he would have been disqualified from such an honour but because he repented, and his heart was so in love with God, he was not disqualified. Truly God does not see as man sees but looks upon the heart.

All this is a great encouragement for us as Christian men. When we lift the breastplate over our shoulders and fit it over our chests, we lock a heart-protector into place. If we have failed, we can cry out from our hearts to God and receive his forgiveness and restoration. We can then make a stand once again with a renewed heart for the ethics of the Kingdom, defined not by our past but by our position.

If we have not failed like David, we can cry out to God from our hearts for his power to enable us to remain faithful in our marriages, families, relationships, workplaces, businesses, finances, churches, and so on. In this he helps us, by giving us the Holy Spirit – the Spirit of holiness – so that we do not fight the world, the flesh and the devil in our own strength alone but with the resources of heaven.

With such resources at work within us we can cultivate purity in our innermost being and live as righteous husbands, fathers, sons, friends, colleagues, workmates, brothers and men. We can, in short, live lives that are conformed to the image of the perfect man, Jesus Christ.

Righting Social Wrongs

Before we leave the subject of righteousness, however, we must understand that the Bible uses this word in two ways when it comes to behaviour. There is first of all what we might call private morality. This is doing the right thing when you're on your own, in the privacy of your own life. Behaving in a righteous way is about making right decisions when no one else is looking, besides God that is. In David's case, it would have meant choosing to look away from Bathsheba as she was bathing and to focus his thoughts instead on whatever is noble, true, Godly and so on. Our lives are composed of many private decisions like these every day - decisions that happen in the secrecy of our own lives. Wearing the breastplate of righteousness means that we protect our hearts against making wrong choices.

It also means that we do the right things not just in private but also in the public arena. In this case, righteousness means behaving in the right way towards my neighbour. Who is my neighbour? Everyone is - especially if he or she is being denied their basic human rights! This kind of public or societal righteousness is what we today refer to as "social justice" - doing the right thing for those whose human rights are being ignored or denied. It means contending for the civil rights of others. It means working hard for the liberation of the oppressed. It means bringing Christ's Jubilee to those enslaved by the demonic powers that work through wicked social systems and structures.

At this point we need to remember that Paul tells us to wear the armour of God and to take our stand against principalities and ruling authorities. These words refer, at least in part, to social structures. As Bible scholar Walter Wink says, they are 'seats of authority, hierarchical systems, ideological justifications, and punitive sanctions which their human incumbents exercise and which transcend these incumbents in both time and power.' These are not 'flesh and blood.' They are ways of thinking and operating designed to exploit vulnerable people. They operate in what Paul calls 'the heavenly realms' and in that sense they transcend those who bow down to them and those who are disempowered by them.

Describing these powers as heavenly realities is of course no license for becoming so heavenly minded that we are no longer any earthly use. In fact, Francis Shaeffer said it implies the exact opposite: 'the primary battle is a spiritual battle in the heavenlies... but it is equally a battle here on earth in our own country, or own communities, our places of work and our schools, and even in our own homes. The spiritual battle has its counterpart in the visible world, in the minds of men and women, and in every area of human culture. In the realm of space and time the heavenly battle is fought on the stage of human history.'

For the Christian man this has sobering implications. It means that we can no longer sit in our seats, in our pews, in our armchairs, passive and indifferent to the cries of the orphan and the widow. Rather it means that we have been commanded to take up and put on the armour of God, including the breastplate of social righteousness. We have been called to guard our hearts against a selfish, privatised spirituality and to allow the Father's love to ignite us with a compassion for the lost, the last and the least.

As a freedom fighter you have been commanded to enter the battle grounds of this world – arenas such as government, media, the arts, education, family, economics, etc – and to promote practical action on behalf of the fatherless, the homeless, the destitute and so forth. Above all, you have been summoned to bring the culture of heaven to those who are experiencing hell on earth, ushering in the reign of the King of Kings in the darkest places.

As Jesus said in Luke 4:18-19:

CHAPTER 5 | GUARDING YOUR HEART

God's Spirit is on me;
  he's chosen me to preach the Message of good news to the poor,
Sent me to announce pardon to prisoners and
  recovery of sight to the blind,
To set the burdened and battered free,
  to announce, "This is God's year to act!"

Fighting for What's Right

If you are a freedom fighter, you will daily choose to go on believing that you are justified in God's sight through what Christ has done. You will constantly rejoice in this Gospel, this Good News, and you will protect your heart with the foundational blessings of this Gospel - that you are made right in the sight of God through what Jesus did for you at Calvary. Even when this Gospel is questioned by humanists and liberalised by theologians, you will keep this over your heart at all times. The true Gospel, the Gospel of Justification, will protect your heart and cover your back at all times.

I want to encourage you every day to remember in the very core of your soul that there is no charge against you in heaven. Your slate has been wiped clean. Your record of wrong decisions and deeds has been erased. There is no accusation against God's children. There is no condemnation for those who are in Christ Jesus.

It is not just that you are no longer in the wrong in God's sight.

By faith, you are now in the right!

Do you see how believing the right thing protects your heart?

But then there is also right behaving. This means choosing to walk the way Jesus walked when He was here on earth as a man. Our model of masculinity and manhood is not taken from the men whom the world idolises and pedestalises. There is no male celebrity on earth who is as worthy of imitation or adoration as Jesus of Nazareth. No, our template of masculinity and manhood is the Son of Man who chose always to do the right thing, both in the private and the public sphere. Our blueprint is the man from heaven who showed us that it is possible, with the help of the Holy Spirit, to do what is right in our own lives and to do what is right for those whose rights have been denied.

You are a freedom fighter.

Believe in the righteousness of Christ.

Behave in the right way in private and in public.

If you do, your heart will always be protected against the subtle and malicious attacks of the enemy and it will always be set on saying and doing what the One and Only Son of God would say and do.

In this way, you will not only stay free.

You will set others free as well.

CHAPTER 5 | GUARDING YOUR HEART

APPLYING THE FREEDOM FIGHTING PRINCIPLES

What am I going to *do* in response to what I've read in this chapter?

Action Point 1

Action Point 2

Action Point 3

What am I going to pray for as a result of what I've read?

Prayer Point 1

Prayer Point 2

Prayer Point 3

PERSONAL TRAINING:

Spend some time considering the questions in the box and bring these to the Lord in prayer.

> To what extent do you value and honour the Good News that you are justified - put in a right standing before God - by faith?
>
> How committed are you to behaving in a way that is radical and right, choosing to live a holy life?
>
> Do you regularly ask yourself what Jesus would say and do when you have important decisions to make?
>
> To what extent do you spend time fighting for the freedom of those whose rights are denied by oppressive social structures?
>
> Towards what kinds of people has your Heavenly Father given you an extraordinary compassion?

CHAPTER 5 | GUARDING YOUR HEART

GROUP TRAINING:

In what ways can you help each other to guard the true Gospel, the Good News, that we are justified by faith?

In what ways does the enemy try to undermine this Good News so that hearts begin to doubt it?

How can you help each other to keep short accounts and to say and do the right things in God's sight?

In what areas as men does the enemy seek to seduce you into saying or doing the wrong things?

How can you help each other as a group of men to fight against the injustices of our times?

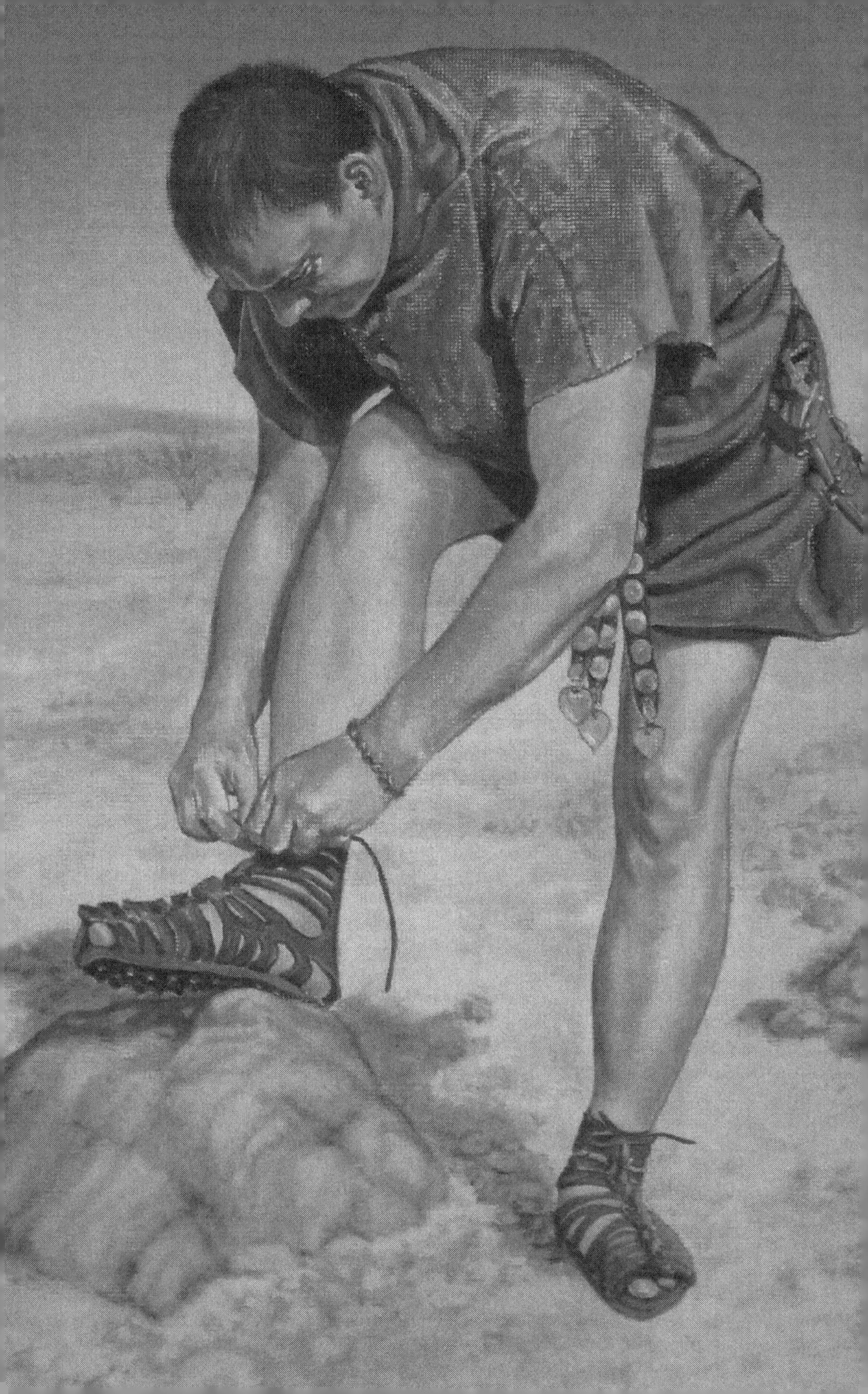

CHAPTER 6

PREPARING YOUR FEET

Have you ever lost your shoes and had to walk somewhere barefoot?

For the Roman soldier, remembering your shoes was crucial. In Paul's day you could tell that someone was a soldier by two items of their clothing. The first was their belt – the decorated single waist belt we described in chapter 3. The second was their caligae or their strapped boots. If a man was walking in the street with a long sleeveless tunic tied by a military balteus you could be almost sure he was a legionary. If you looked at his footwear and saw that he was also sporting a pair of *caligae*, you could be absolutely certain.

What were these boots like? They were heavy-duty half-boots with iron-nailed soles. Their soles, in fact, were remarkably advanced. These nailing patterns gave support to the heel, arch and ball of the soldier's feet and allowed for considerable grip and manoeuvrability. In his book on the *Roman Legionary 58 BC – AD 69* (the source for some of the material on the Roman soldier's armour in these chapters), Ross Cowan says these heavy sandals were 'the precursors of the sole patterns on modern training shoes.'

Although there is some debate about when exactly these *caligae* became standard issue in the Roman army, we do know that by the time of the Emperor Augustus' reign these boots had become the regular footwear for Roman legionaries. Along with the jangle of the metal on their belts, it was the distinctive crunching sound of these iron-nailed shoes on stone streets and roads that would have indicated the imminence of Roman soldiers.

With that in mind, we return to Ephesians 6. When the Apostle Paul told us to dress for spiritual warfare, the first item he mentions is the belt of truth and the second the breastplate of righteousness. Now he turns his attention to our footwear.

Stand therefore, having girded your waist with truth, having put on the breastplate of righteousness, and having shod your feet with the preparation of the gospel of peace.

In the original Greek text Paul says 'having fitted your feet with the readiness of the gospel of peace'. Although he doesn't specifically mention them here, Paul was thinking of the caligae worn by the Roman legionary.

At the same time the emphasis on feet rather than actual footwear suggests that Paul also has an Old Testament quotation in mind. We are referring of course to Isaiah 52.7, *'how beautiful on the mountains are the feet of him who brings good news.'*

Freedom fighters wear Gospel shoes!

Good News of Victory

This brings us to the words 'good news'. Paul says that we are to fit our feet with the readiness or preparation of the gospel of peace. The word 'gospel' means 'good news' and was used in the Roman Empire when heralds ran into cities to announce good news about the Emperor's victories in far off lands. 'Good news! Good news!' they would shout on the streets of Rome. 'Our great Emperor has conquered our enemies. Peace has come. We are free!"

What then did Paul mean by the 'readiness' or 'preparation' of the gospel of peace? To answer this we must go back in the letter to Ephesians 2.14-18 where Paul announces that Christ is our peace. Christ has made peace both vertically and horizontally through his death on the Cross. In other words, he has reconciled men and women to God and has also reconciled men and women to each other. The greatest illustration of the latter was the fact that both Jews and Gentiles, who had formerly always been at enmity with each other, had been reconciled through the Cross and were now worshipping the Father through Jesus in the presence of the Holy Spirit. The dividing wall had come crashing down and what was deemed impossible – Jews and non-Jews loving each other – had become possible thanks to what Jesus had done at Calvary.

In light of this, we can see how the Gospel of Jesus Christ truly is about peace because it is the only force on earth that brings an end to war. What human politics is always trying to achieve with limited results and over many years, Christ achieves with extraordinary results and over a very short space of time. He brings peace.

At the same time, this new peace has ironically intensified the spiritual warfare in our planet. The devil is now furious because he knows that all his attempts to divide people from God and each other were exposed and disarmed at Calvary.

But this is not all!

The devil's tactics are also confounded by the church. The church, now filled with people who love rather than hate each other, is a reminder not only of the devil's past defeat at the Cross but also his future demise at the last judgment, where cosmic harmony will be established in and through Jesus Christ.

No wonder the devil hates the church just as he hates Christ!

Unbreakable Unity

We can see then that the Gospel of peace has resulted in an increase in spiritual warfare. This is of course a paradox. The peace achieved through Christ's death, resurrection and ascension has resulted in the dark powers of the universe fighting even more ferociously. Even though Christ rules with supreme authority above these powers, and so indeed do we as his followers, these hostile entities still attempt to cause mayhem in the world and especially in the church, where their favourite tactic is to try to divide and conquer.

Think about it for a moment. Why is there so much division in the church? Surely if Christ has brought us a supernatural peace, there should be harmony everywhere. Often times there is, but there are also times when the church becomes racially divided, or when churches rise up in pride and speak divisively of their superiority over other churches.

Why does this happen?

Part of the answer lies in the foolish choices made by those of us who all too fallibly follow Christ. But there is also a larger and more sinister reason. The truth is the devil wants to divide the church as much as possible because a united church defuses his powers but a fractured church gives him space in which to cause havoc.

This is why Paul tells the Christians in Ephesus to be very careful not to get angry with each other, to slander one another, to become bitter with one another. This kind of divisive behaviour, so often flowing from peoples' mouths, grieves the Holy Spirit and gives the devil a foothold in the church.

See what Paul says in Ephesians 4:25-28:

Therefore, putting away lying, "Let each one of you speak truth with his neighbour," for we are members of one another. Be angry, and do not sin: do not let the sun go down on your wrath, nor give place to the devil.

So here's what Paul meant by the 'readiness of the Gospel of peace': he means 'the state of maximum readiness for standing firm in the battle – a battle which has been intensified as a result of

CHAPTER 6 | PREPARING YOUR FEET

the gospel of Christ's peace being preached.'

Freedom fighters are to prepare themselves every day of their lives to stand firm, wearing their caligae at all times in preparation for withstanding the onslaught of dark powers bent on the division and destruction of the world and the church.

Every freedom fighter is to have their feet fitted with these spiritual army boots, and each one of us is called to make sure that our nail-studded soles are gripping hard into the ground won for us by Christ himself.

We are not to be found unprepared.

We are not to yield a metre to the enemy.

We are to stand firm and together, like holy legionaries, in ranks of unbreakable unity.

Blessed are the Peacemakers

What then are the implications for us as freedom fighters? It is here that we must recognise the importance of the context of the armour of God passage in Ephesians 6. In the previous chapter of Ephesians, Paul has turned his attention to the issue of how we should walk. This part of his letter begins in Ephesians 5.15-16 with the words:

See then that you walk circumspectly, not as fools but as wise, redeeming the time, because the days are evil.

In the verses that follow, Paul addresses a number of situations in which the Christian must intentionally resolve to walk in a holy, Christ-like way – in a way that befits the dearly loved children of a perfect Father.

The first context that Paul addresses is the home.

In Ephesians 5.22-30, Paul exhorts Christian wives to submit to their husbands and Christian husbands to lay down their lives for their wives. In Ephesians 6.1-4, Paul continues to apply his holiness code to the home by addressing children and their parents. Children are to obey their parents, in accordance with the Commandments, and fathers are to resist the temptation to exasperate their children.

From the home, Paul now moves to the workplace. In Ephesians 6.5-9, he urges Christian employees to be loyal and hardworking and Christian employers to be fair and kind.

Bondservants, be obedient to those who are your masters according to the flesh, with fear and trembling, in sincerity of heart, as to Christ; not with eyeservice, as men-pleasers, but as bondservants of Christ, doing the will of God from the heart, with good will doing service, as to the Lord, and not to men, knowing that whatever good anyone does, he will receive the same from the Lord, whether he is a slave or free. And you, masters, do the same things to them, giving up threatening, knowing that your own Master also is in heaven, and there is no partiality with Him.

All this has radical implications for freedom fighters at every level.

It means that I commit to being a peacemaker in my marriage, turning my armour against every demonic attack on my marriage, not against my wife by engaging in words and deeds that are combative and destructive.

It means that I commit to being a peacemaker in my role as a father, turning my armour against every demonic attack on my family, not against my children by exasperating them with aggressive discipline and harsh words.

It means that I commit to being a peacemaker in my role as a member of my local church, turning my armour against every demonic attack on my church family not against my spiritual fathers and mothers, or against my brothers and sisters in Christ.

CHAPTER 6 | PREPARING YOUR FEET

It means that I commit to being a peacemaker in my workplace and my job, turning my armour against every demonic attack on the company or organization I serve, not against my bosses or fellow employees.

It means that I commit to being a peacemaker in this war-torn and unjust world, turning my armour against every demonic attack that comes through social structures that oppress people, not against those who are the victims of war and injustice.

I prepare my feet with peace every day of my life and work for peace in my marriage, in my family, in my church, in my workplace, in the world at large. In this way I prove that I am an adopted son of God. Jesus said, "Blessed are the peacemakers for they shall be called the sons of God." My daily choice to be a peacemaker displays my true identity as a son of God. Those who are truly sons of God use their armour against the darkness not against each other.

Going the Extra Mile

Is there ever a case for freedom fighters to use violence to enforce peace? In answering this we need to remember that while there is occasionally a case to be made for what is called a "just war", the true freedom fighter is a man of peace. We are citizens of another world. We belong to the Kingdom of heaven. Whenever we are faced by great darkness, we must seek to respond with the peace-loving strategies of the culture of heaven, not with the aggressive and violent practices of this world. As Jesus said in Matthew 5:38-41, as he outlined the non-violent path of peace that he expected his disciples to take: *"You have heard the law that says the punishment must match the injury: 'An eye for an eye, and a tooth for a tooth. But I say, do not resist an evil person! If someone slaps you on the right cheek, offer the other cheek also. If you are sued in court and your shirt is taken from you, give your coat, too.*

If a soldier demands that you carry his gear for a mile, carry it two miles."

Is Jesus encouraging us to be spineless here? Bible scholar Walter Wink says no. Taking the third of the commands – about going two miles instead of one - he explains that this saying must be understood against the backcloth of Israel under Roman occupation. In such a climate Jewish men were often forced to carry the equipment of the Roman soldiers. We know that Roman legionaries used to wear heavy backpacks which contained his spare clothes, food, cooking utensils and mess kit. These weighed about 30lbs. Legionaries would often get tired and order local men to carry their packs. While the locals regarded this as thoroughly degrading, the soldiers would see it as one of the rewards for being the occupying power.

Roman officers accepted that their soldiers could do this but also stipulated that they should not take it too far so they restricted the length that a Jewish man could carry the pack to just one mile. It is this rule that Jesus is referring to here. Far from telling his followers to resist with violence, he tells them to carry the pack an extra mile - one mile further than the Roman officers permitted. This is a thoroughly subversive command and one that would have turned the tables on the Roman legionary who had ordered you to take his pack. By refusing to return it after the statutory one mile, and bearing it for an extra mile, you would have caused your oppressor to break the rules. In the process, a non-violent response would have got the victimizer in trouble with his commanding officer, turning him into the victim. The one shaming would have become the one shamed, without a sword being drawn!

All this shows how radical Jesus' much misunderstood teaching was on 'going the extra mile.' It is the opposite of how human cultures operate. It is not an example of what Walter Wink calls 'the myth of redemptive violence' – the view that you can only redeem your situation of oppression by resorting to violence (a mindset illustrated in many popular stories and films). That is not the way of love. The way of love is non-violent but non-violent does not mean inactive or stupid.

When Paul tells us to prepare our feet with the Gospel of peace, he is not exhorting men to take up physical, literal arms and to resort to violence. No, his way is the way of Christ and the way of Christ is the way opened up by the Gospel of peace. Far from encouraging militant aggression or military action, Paul is therefore rousing us to stand firm in support of the Good News that Christ brings peace between man and God, and between peoples and nations, and he does that through non-violent and extreme love - the love that Jesus displayed when he went to the Cross and suffered at the hands of Roman soldiers.

The Call to Suffer

Sometimes, of course, this means that we freedom fighters will have to suffer but in accepting and enduring this, we model the ministry of reconciliation contained within the Gospel – a peace-making ministry of suffering that is the furthest remove from the peace-enforcing tactics of the Roman Empire.

Here is Paul in Ephesians 2.14-18:

For He [Christ] Himself is our peace, who has made both one, and has broken down the middle wall of separation, having abolished in His flesh the enmity, that is, the law of commandments contained in ordinances, so as to create in Himself one new man from the two, thus making peace, and that He might reconcile them both to God in one body through the cross, thereby putting to death the enmity. And He came and preached peace to you who were afar off and to those who were near. For through Him we both have access by one Spirit to the Father.

Christ is the Prince of Peace and the Peacemaker. In fact, he is the personification and embodiment of Peace. He is the Shalom of Heaven – the one who reconciles warring tribes, nations and people through his death.

Yes, through his death.

It is through the suffering of his flesh upon a Roman Cross that Christ brings peace. It is through his shed blood that enmity is destroyed and unity is established.

This, then, has implications for freedom fighters. Paul has already urged Christian husbands to love their wives as Christ loved his bride the church. This means a lifestyle of self-sacrificial love. It means that there is a cost to be endured and a price to be paid, both within the home, the church, the workplace and beyond. Freedom fighters are ready to suffer whatever it takes within the family and the workplace to get both family members and work colleagues to turn their armour outwards towards the powers rather than inwards towards each other. It means that freedom fighters are prepared to imitate Jesus and to suffer a moment in the flesh so that the already-won victory might be enjoyed forever.

And this ultimately is all about victory.

The Shoes of Victory

As the freedom fighter wears his spiritual *caligae*, he knows that Christ has already won the decisive battle against the powers of darkness. The freedom fighter is seated with Christ far above these powers. He is therefore a man of victory. He can always bring the peace of the Cross into every situation, as long as he is wearing his shoes of peace.

The freedom fighter is therefore on the winning side!

Listen to the Apostle Paul's famous conclusion to Romans chapter 8 (verses 35-39):

Who shall separate us from the love of Christ? Shall trouble or hardship or persecution or famine or nakedness or danger or sword?

CHAPTER 6 | PREPARING YOUR FEET

As it is written:

"For your sake we face death all day long; we are considered as sheep to be slaughtered."

No, in all these things we are more than conquerors through him who loved us. For I am convinced that neither death nor life, neither angels nor demons, neither the present nor the future, nor any powers, neither height nor depth, nor anything else in all creation, will be able to separate us from the love of God that is in Christ Jesus our Lord.

Paul doesn't deny that freedom fighters have to endure suffering. In fact, he lists seven types of suffering that we can expect: trouble, hardship, persecution, famine, nakedness, danger and even the sword. But he makes it clear that none of these has the power to separate us from the divine love and that in all of these things we can be victorious.

The word Paul uses here is the word 'conqueror'. This is in fact a verb in the Greek, *hupernikao*. It means to go beyond mere conquering! It means to be hyper-triumphant – 'super-achievers', to use today's terminology. Notice the little word *nikao*. *Nikao* means "to conquer". *Nike* is the noun form and it means victory. In the ancient world, *Nike* was a Greek winged goddess – an attendant of Zeus, the father of the gods, and a deity associated with strength and triumph. One of the best known athletic shoes in the world today is the *Nike* brand. The word denotes speed and success. The tagline associated with the brand is, 'Just Do it!'

For the freedom fighter, the shoes of readiness are a critical piece of his kit. He has a pair of heaven's *caligae* - shoes with extraordinary grip that are ideal for standing your ground when the terrain is rough and the winds are strong. On these shoes, heaven's brand is imprinted in the logo of a Cross – the symbol of Christ's comprehensive defeat of the powers and conquest over the devil. With these shoes, the freedom fighter is ever-ready to respond to the demonic retaliation provoked by the proclamation throughout the streets of the world, 'good news! Good news! Jesus Christ has conquered all our enemies and peace has come.'

With these shoes, we can be more than conquerors.

We can encourage one another with the words, 'Just Do it!'

We can be freedom fighters in a war-torn world, bringing the Gospel of Peace into our homes, workplaces and cities.

CHAPTER 6 | PREPARING YOUR FEET

APPLYING THE FREEDOM FIGHTING PRINCIPLES

What am I going to *do* in response to what I've read in this chapter?

Action Point 1

___

Action Point 2

___

Action Point 3

___

What am I going to pray for as a result of what I've read?

Prayer Point 1

___

Prayer Point 2

___

Prayer Point 3

___

PERSONAL TRAINING:

Spend some time considering the questions in the box and bring these to the Lord in prayer.

Consider these areas of your life and influence as a freedom fighter

- WORLD
- WORKPLACE
- CHURCH
- HOME

What do you need to do to be more prepared to be a peacemaker in these spheres of influence?

In which of these contexts do you need to redirect your armour outwards towards the enemy?

In what ways do you need to bring your thoughts and words into line with the code of conduct in Ephesians 4:25-28?

Is there anyone in any of these four circles of influence that you need to forgive from your heart?

CHAPTER 6 | PREPARING YOUR FEET

GROUP TRAINING:

Consider these areas of your life and influence as freedom fighters

- WORLD
- WORKPLACE
- CHURCH
- HOME

Where is the spirit of division most evident in these contexts right now?

How can you stand together as men to war against the enemy and bring the peace of God into these situations?

What can you together to be ministers of reconciliation in these areas?

Are there ways you can "walk the extra mile?"

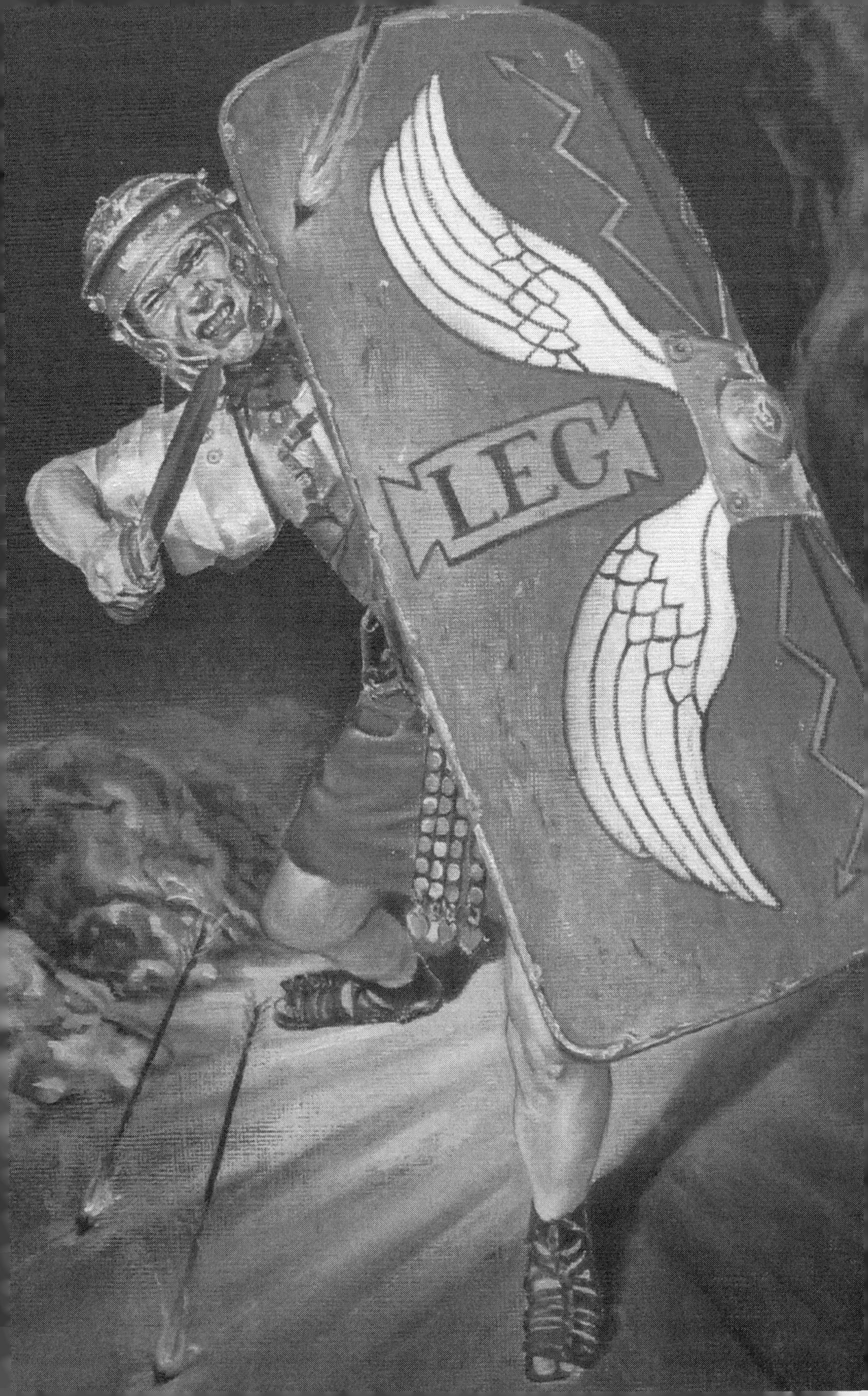
LEG

CHAPTER 7

LIFTING YOUR SHIELD

Every freedom fighter needs a shield to defend themselves against the fiery arrows that the enemy sends against us. Good thing then that our Heavenly Father has equipped us with the shield of faith - the fourth item in the armour of God in Ephesians 6.

How strong is your faith shield today?

Freedom fighters need shields that are robust if they are to get free, stay free and set free those who are held captive by the enemy.

We are in a fierce battle and we face an exceedingly violent and insidious enemy. If we do not pay careful attention to our faith, stewarding and strengthening it every day, we may find ourselves wounded in the fray.

However, if we look after our faith and raise it against the enemy, in close ranks with other freedom fighting brothers, we will shield both ourselves and our loved ones and enjoy the glorious freedom of the children of God.

An Offensive Weapon

Given that this item of the soldier's armour is so important, let's take a look at it more closely. As we've been realizing in this manual, the armour of God passage in Ephesians 6 is inspired by Paul's frequent encounters with Roman legionaries. What then did the Roman soldier's shield look like in Paul's day? Here is

Polybius' description:

"The Roman panoply consists firstly of a shield (scutum), the convex surface of which measures two and a half feet in width and four feet in length, the thickness at the rim being a palm's breadth. It is made of two planks glued together, the outer surface being then covered first with canvas and then with calf-skin. Its upper and lower rims are strengthened by an iron edging which protects it from descending blows and from injury when rested on the ground. It also has an iron boss (umbo) fixed to it which turns aside the most formidable blows of stones, pikes, and heavy missiles in general."

Notice how Polybius puts the shield first in the list. It was clearly of primary importance in the Roman soldier's equipment.

What more can we say about this shield?

In the time of Caesar Augustus, the standard shield of the legionary was rectangular in shape. It was considerably lighter than its predecessor, weighing less than 13 lbs instead of the previous 22 lbs. It was only 5mm thick and was held by its horizontal grip with a straight arm. It had iron edges and an iron, pointed boss in the centre. This was used with lethal effect as a ramming device when the front rank of a century of legionaries charged and punched violently into their opponents, shouting as they did. The boss would often cause the enemy to become unbalanced and fall over, whereupon they would be dispatched with the sword. In this light, we can see that the often made remark that the sword is the only offensive weapon in Ephesians 6 is way off the mark. The scutum or shield was just as much an offensive as a defensive weapon.

On the outside of the shield, the wooden surface was covered by both canvas and the hides of animals adding an extra layer of protection. These were doused in water before every battle. Whenever the enemy applied pitch or tow to their arrows and ignited them, the soaked skins on the front of the legionaries' shields would not only absorb the blow, they would also extinguish the burning arrows. These burning arrows were known as malleoli and they were a constant threat to the legions. However, the legionary's shield was more than a match for them. The shield of faith is more than a match for the fiery arrows of the devil as well.

Quenching Fiery Arrows

Paul tells us 'above all' put on the shield of faith. "Above all" in Greek is en pasin which could also mean "in all circumstances" or "in addition to all these." If it means "in all circumstances", then the freedom fighter should make sure that his shield is in place in every situation in his life, from his home to the workplace. If it means "in addition to these other items," the freedom fighter must not neglect to put his shield in place after tightening his belt, donning his breastplate and putting on his shoes. As Ephesians 6.14-16 says:

Stand therefore, having girded your waist with truth, having put on the breastplate of righteousness, and having shod your feet with the preparation of the gospel of peace; above all, taking the shield of faith with which you will be able to quench all the fiery darts of the wicked one.

What can we learn about the warfare in which the freedom fighter is called to participate? What can we also learn about the freedom fighter's battle tactics?

From the verses above we learn that freedom fighters are belted soldiers, with strong breastplates and nail-soled boots, who raise their water-soaked shields to the fiery arrows sent against them. These arrows are sent by the devil, described here as the 'evil one' (poneros). With this shield raised, either in front or above the body, the burning arrows of the enemy – not just some of them but all (panta) - can be countered and comprehensively neutralised. As Paul says, if freedom fighters take up their shields, then they will be able (future tense) to protect their lives against every fiery assault sent by the wicked one.

In light of this I want to encourage you to see yourselves as spiritual legionaries standing in tight ranks, with long rectangular shields raised in front or to the side (depending on whether you are in the front or on the outer edges of the formation) or above your heads (if you are positioned in the centre).

It is a graphic, rousing and radical picture.

Defenders of the Faith

In 1 John 5:4-5 we read this:

For whatever is born of God overcomes the world. And this is the victory [nike] that has overcome the world - our faith. Who is he who overcomes the world, but he who believes that Jesus is the Son of God?

If we are to conquer what the world, the flesh and the devil throw at us, then we need faith. Without faith there is no victory. With faith, we can all overcome.

So what is "faith?"

At the most general level, faith is quite simply the God-given capacity to believe with confidence those things that are not seen by the natural eye.

Put more succinctly, faith means believing what you cannot yet see.

Think about it. We cannot see Jesus at the moment. He is alive in his resurrection life but he is not visible to our eyes. This doesn't mean that he isn't real. Jesus Christ is real, resurrected and reigning. Even though we cannot see him in all of his royal and heavenly majesty, we believe that he rules over all the powers of the cosmos and that one day he will return on the clouds with unparalleled splendour. As we wait for this momentous day, we believe that Jesus

CHAPTER 7 | LIFTING YOUR SHIELD

is God's One and Only Son and we proclaim that even though the world may be in a forlorn mess, Jesus Christ is still on the throne of God in the heavenly realms.

While faith is to believe what you cannot yet see, the reward of faith is eventually to see what we currently believe.

So what did Paul mean by the shield of "faith"? Remember what we have learned so far: all the items of armour are representations of both what we are called to believe and how we are supposed to behave. As freedom fighters, we are called to believe the right thing and behave in the right way. We cannot believe any old thing about Jesus. We cannot give into the ideas of pluralism, for example, and say that Jesus is just one way among a plurality of ways to God. No, we must ground our faith in what the Bible says, not in what men and women say, however clever they may be. We must keep on defending the truth that Jesus is THE Way not "a way". We must keep emphasizing the little word "THE." That is called raising the shield of faith.

Likewise, when it comes to behaviour, we cannot give into the ideas of relativism, for example, and say that every way of behaving is relatively right and no way of behaving is absolutely right or wrong. No, we must ground our ideas of how to behave in what the Bible says not what the media or the universities say. We must always look to be faithful to what Jesus would want us to say and do in every situation, even if it is a battle and it costs us. That is what it means to raise the shield of faith.

It is impossible to be a true freedom fighter in this world without lifting your shield of faith every day.

This means being full of faith in the uniqueness and supremacy of Jesus Christ.

It also means being faithful to how Jesus wants you to conduct yourself.

Faith is Faith in Christ

Let's look at both of these dimensions of faith in as little more detail.

Let's first of all look at what it means to raise the shield of faith in Christ.

As far as the Apostle Paul is concerned, when he talks about the shield of faith, he doesn't mean any old faith. He means faith in Jesus Christ. Faith for Paul means faith in the one who is seated in the heavenly places far above every principality, every title, everything. It means continuing to believe that Jesus Christ is the Lord of Heaven and Earth and that at His mighty name, every knee will one day bow to the glory of God, our Abba Father.

Let's look at how Paul uses the word 'faith' in Ephesians to prove the point. Here are some of the references:

I heard of your faith in the Lord Jesus

[Ephesians 1:15].

For by grace you have been saved through faith, and that not of yourselves; it is the gift of God, not of works, lest anyone should boast.

[Ephesians 2.8-9]

... that Christ may dwell in your hearts through faith

[Ephesians 3.17]

... till we all come to the unity of the faith and of the knowledge of the Son of God, to a perfect man, to the measure of the stature of the fullness of Christ

[Ephesians 4:13]

From these examples you can see that for Paul faith is inseparable from the person of Jesus Christ. For Paul, faith is faith in the Lord Jesus. Yes, I said "Lord." This means more than just "master." In Latin the word is *dominus* and in Greek the word is *kurios*. To believe and proclaim that "Jesus is Lord" is to believe and proclaim that he is the ruling authority above every other ruling authority – including the Roman Emperor.

For Paul, faith is what saves a person. It saves them *from* a shameful, sin-centred life with all its destructive and disastrous consequences and saves them *to* a Christ-centred life with all its outrageous rewards, such as the matchless honour of being seated with Christ above the powers of this present age – a position which is to be enjoyed now.

For Paul, faith is what enables a person to have more than just an intellectual assent to truth. Faith is what enables a person to enjoy the indescribable privilege of having Jesus – the Lord of the Universe – dwelling in our hearts. By faith, Jesus Christ the Risen King takes up residence in our lives and rules with love over all that we are.

For Paul, faith is faith in Jesus as the Son of God. In his eyes, the Christian is a man or a woman who is wholly committed to spiritual maturity, growing into someone who truly believes that Jesus is God's One and Only Son, one who truly *knows* that Jesus is God's Son – not just cognitively but also affectionately.

The Son of God

Please remember how radical this was in its original context. In the Roman world, the Emperor was regarded as "son of god." Some of the Emperors after Caesar Augustus even believed this about themselves. In the language of the Roman Empire – which was of course Latin – the exact words were *divi filius*. For a Christian in the Roman Empire of Paul's day, raising the shield of faith therefore meant something extremely dangerous. It meant promoting a conviction that Jesus alone is worthy of the title "Son of God."

This is radical! When the Roman centurion at the foot of the Cross declares that Jesus is truly the son of God (Mark 15.3) we may be guilty of underestimating the significance of this confession. The Roman centurion would have known all too well that "son of God" was a title reserved for his Emperor. Yet, seeing the extraordinary fortitude of the dying Messiah in front of him, faith rises up in him and out of his mouth comes a pronouncement that represents a surprising and potent challenge to the dark powers influencing the Imperial Cult. He says that Jesus, the crucified Nazarene, deserves the title 'son of God.' Life for the centurion, if he continued to trust in Christ and remain in the Roman army, would not have been easy from this moment on.

Freedom fighters need to get radical too!

The Lord of All!

For Paul, faith in Christ meant believing, confessing and proclaiming not only that Jesus Christ is the Son of God but also "Lord."

Reading the start of 1 Corinthians 12, we may wonder why it is that Paul says that it is only possible to confess that "Jesus is Lord" except with the help of the Holy Spirit. As he prepares to launch into a paragraph about the gifts of the Holy Spirit, he says this:

Now concerning spiritual gifts, brethren, I do not want you to be ignorant: You know that you were Gentiles, carried away to these dumb idols, however you were led. Therefore I make known to you that no one speaking by the Spirit of God calls Jesus accursed, and no one can say that Jesus is Lord except by the Holy Spirit.

[1 Corinthians 12.1-3]

Surely it is a relatively easy thing to open one's mouth and say the words, "Jesus is Lord!" Yes, maybe so, at least in the comfortable social context in which many of us live today but this was not so

CHAPTER 7 | LIFTING YOUR SHIELD

in the first century when confessing that Jesus as Lord was an extraordinarily dangerous thing to say. Only someone filled with the Spirit of God could have the boldness to do that. Such a confession could never have been the product of natural resolve. It would have to be supernaturally inspired.

When a person became a Christian in the Roman Empire of Paul's day they did so because something momentous had happened in their hearts. They had come to believe with absolute certainty that Jesus of Nazareth, crucified on a Roman Cross, had not only died for their sins but been raised from the dead. This heart-felt conviction then produced a vocal declaration. People who owned the fact that Jesus was alive forevermore realised that he was Lord in a way that a mortal Emperor could never be. They accordingly declared with their mouths that Jesus Christ is Lord. This is why Paul says in Romans 10.9:

If you confess with your mouth the Lord Jesus and believe in your heart that God has raised Him from the dead, you will be saved.

In the New International Version this is even clearer:

If you confess with your mouth, "Jesus is Lord," and believe in your heart that God raised him from the dead, you will be saved.

Believing in the resurrection of Jesus therefore released a powerful confession in his Lordship. "He's alive" led to "He is Lord!"

In a world where Caesar was regarded and confessed as *dominus* (Latin), this was radical. Paul knew that raising the shield of faith meant confronting and engaging the dark powers that influenced millions of Roman citizens to confess that Caesar was *dominus*. Declaring Christ's Lordship therefore meant taking the shield of faith and ramming it into the ranks of the enemy. It meant counter-cultural courage.

Isn't it time for freedom fighters to get radical?

The Prince of Peace

The freedom fighter is convinced not only that Jesus is Son of God and Lord but also that He is our Peace. He is the one whose death on the Cross has brought about reconciliation both vertically and horizontally. Vertically, Christ's death has brought an end to the hostility between man and God – a hostility arising solely out of man's sinfulness and rebellion – and produced a lasting peace, a *shalom* in which man can now know God as his friend. Horizontally, Christ's death has resulted in the possibility of warring tribes and nations finding peace with each other. At the foot of the Cross, enemies become friends. This is 'Gospel!' It is Good News! Christ, the Prince of Peace, has made peace and given us the ministry of reconciliation. He has given us the opportunity and the resources to proclaim the Gospel of peace and to lead people whom the politicians could never unite into a harmony that astounds the world and confounds the devil.

Remember that in the Roman Empire, the word gospel (*evangelion* in Greek) meant "glad tidings." It was a word used when there was good news to report concerning the activities of the Roman Emperor. On an inscription in Priene, dating from 9BC, we find these words about the Emperor Augustus' birthday: "the birthday of the god was the beginning of the glad tidings of joy on account of him." For the Roman citizen, Augustus' birthday was worth celebrating as "good news" because the Emperor had brought peace to the world and this Emperor was regarded as a god (small "g").

Remember, however, that the methods used by Caesar (which means "Emperor") were altogether different from the methods advocated by Christ. In Caesar's case, peace was established by brute force. It was not the result of negotiation but of occupation. It arose out of destruction not out of diplomacy. Indeed, the Roman historian Tacitus quotes some words of the British chieftain called

CHAPTER 7 | LIFTING YOUR SHIELD

Calgacus. Commenting on the Roman way, Calgacus comments that "where they made destitution, they call it peace." This is of course a paradox, one highlighted by the location of the altar of peace in Rome. This ironically stood on Mars Hill (Mars being the Roman god of war). In the Roman mind, peace comes as a result of war.

How different this is from the way of Christ. Christ brought peace not by utilizing the victimizing forces of the Roman Empire but by submitting to them in loving, subversive and non-violent resistance at the Cross. As Paul says in Colossians 1.19-22:

It pleased the Father that in Him all the fullness should dwell, and by Him to reconcile all things to Himself, by Him, whether things on earth or things in heaven, having made peace through the blood of His cross. And you, who once were alienated and enemies in your mind by wicked works, yet now He has reconciled in the body of His flesh through death.

Jesus Christ is truly the Peace Bringer. No wonder, when Christ was born, the angels announced the "glad tidings" (Gospel) that Jesus was the Saviour and that he was bringing peace on earth. From a political view this was a direct confrontation to the good news that Caesar has brought peace to the earth through violence. Far from being a safe and quaint event, the nativity was accordingly a declaration of war.

There was truly danger in the manger!

Isn't it time for freedom fighters to get radical?

The World's Saviour

Faith in Christ also involves believing and proclaiming that Jesus is 'Saviour.' This was at the very heart of Jesus' name and it was at the very heart of his purpose. Jesus came to save people from their sins. Even the Samaritan inhabitants of Sychar understood this. After encountering Jesus at the well they declared that he was "the Saviour of the world" (John 4.42).

Confessing that Jesus the Jew was the global Saviour was no trivial thing, especially in the Roman Empire. The Roman Emperor was called "Saviour" and indeed "Saviour of the world." By bringing order and peace to a chaotic and unruly planet, the Emperor was regarded and revered as the world's rescuer, deliverer and saviour.

This ability to bring peace to the earth was understood by Roman citizens over time as an attribute of divinity. Surely only a god or a demigod had the power and authority to achieve such a colossal task? Surely only a deity could bring about a new world order? No wonder the cult of the Emperor developed into a full blown religion.

In the Roman Empire of Paul's day, there were two forces that kept the conquered world in a state of enforced peace. The first was of course the Roman legions. This was a physical means of enforcing *Pax Romana*, Roman Peace. The second was the growing Imperial Cult, a cult which vanquished territories were quickly compelled to adopt. This was more of a spiritual means of enforcing peace. Within this cult, people began to be seduced by the deception that Caesar was Lord of the world. Conquered peoples everywhere therefore began to call him Saviour. This deception was a political masterstroke. If occupied peoples could be persuaded to acknowledge Caesar as Saviour and Lord, then there would be far less need to keep them in line through the use of Roman soldiers. All that was needed was blind devotion to the Emperor.

It was in this context that the first Christians found themselves. They came to acknowledge that Jesus is the Saviour of the World and in making this declaration they immediately ran into conflict and trouble. Faith in Christ as the Saviour of the world brought them into intense spiritual conflict with the prevailing dark powers in their world, which were Roman imperialistic powers. Faith in

CHAPTER 7 | LIFTING YOUR SHIELD

Christ therefore required immense courage. Standing for Jesus in a world of Emperor-worship meant raising a faith-shield to the deifying forces which had inspired and now sustained the Imperial Cult. No wonder Paul said 'above all, take up the shield of faith.'

It was radical then.

It is radical now.

Isn't it time for freedom fighters to get radical?

The Coming King!

It is impossible to leave this topic without mentioning that faith in Christ has a future tense. It is not just a matter of believing certain things to be true in the past - that, for example, Jesus Christ was raised from the dead and thereby vindicated as the Son of God. Nor is it merely a matter of continuing to believe in the present that Jesus of Nazareth is the only human being in history who is also divine, and therefore worthy of titles like Saviour and Lord. It is also a matter of looking ahead to the future and trusting with a God-given certainty that Jesus Christ will one day come back to the planet that he visited and that when he does he will be acknowledged for who he really is – the King of Kings and the Lord of lords - the Lord who is far above others who are called "lord", including Caesar.

Faith accordingly has a future focus. It looks forward to the last things of history. It gazes ahead to the future events prophesied in the Bible, including – using Tolkien's words – "the Return of the King." In other words, faith in Christ means faith in the Second Coming of Jesus Christ on the last day of history.

Here we must give attention to one of Paul's most creative terms for the Second Coming, namely *parousia*, a Greek word that can be translated as "appearing, arrival, advent, presence, or coming, always with reference to the return of Jesus.

Perhaps the most detailed description of how Paul saw this parousia is in a magnificent and reassuring passage in 1 Thessalonians 4:13-18:

I do not want you to be ignorant, brethren, concerning those who have fallen asleep, lest you sorrow as others who have no hope. For if we believe that Jesus died and rose again, even so God will bring with Him those who sleep in Jesus. For this we say to you by the word of the Lord, that we who are alive and remain until **the coming of the Lord** *will by no means precede those who are asleep. For the Lord Himself will descend from heaven with a shout, with the voice of an archangel, and with the trumpet of God. And the dead in Christ will rise first. Then we who are alive and remain shall be caught up together with them in the clouds to meet the Lord in the air. And thus we shall always be with the Lord. Therefore comfort one another with these words.*

Notice the words underlined "the coming of the Lord." The word translated "coming" in the New King James Version is *parousia*. Paul uses this word four times in 1 Thessalonians and always and only with reference to the Lord Jesus. For Paul, the final, climactic act of history is the *parousia* of Jesus Christ who is Lord. Why is this so significant? The answer is because the word *parousia* was used in Paul's day of the arrival of the Emperor on a visit to one of his colonies or provinces. Before this happened, roads were repaired so that the Emperor could travel comfortably. Crowds assembled to pay homage as processions of white-clothed men and women marched ahead of the Emperor to the sound of many trumpets. In some cities even advent coins were minted for the occasion.

In plundering this term, Paul brilliantly exploits the idea of an Imperial visit by applying it to Jesus Christ. The future return of Jesus Christ on this earth is far more dramatic and significant than any sudden appearance of the Emperor in a Roman colony. It is Christ who is the true Lord of the world not Caesar. As soon as

CHAPTER 7 | LIFTING YOUR SHIELD

Christ the Lord returns, all things will be gathered together in one in the person of Jesus Christ – things in heaven as well as earth (Ephesians 1:10). This must have inspired first century Christians with hope. In the midst of Roman persecution, they could look at the powers behind their oppression and say with Paul, "one day there is going to be a *parousia* that will put an end to all this – a *parousia* that will far outshine anything that the Emperors have produced. When that happens, every demonic power will be annihilated forever and every social manifestation of those powers will be brought down, never to rise again."

No wonder Paul could say to his readers in 1 Thessalonians 4, "comfort one another with these words." When Christians in the first century raised the shield of faith, they fortified themselves with the inspiring truth that Jesus Christ is the true Lord of the universe and he is one day going to make a *parousia* which will terminate the persecuting powers, permanently. Faith in Christ therefore has a future orientation. It leads the Christian away from saying, "look what the world is coming to," and draws them instead to the place of faith – the place where they can say with confidence, "Look who's coming to the world."

That's radical.

Isn't it time for freedom fighters to get radical?

Faithful unto Death

When Paul told us to lift the shield of faith he was telling us to defend our belief in Christ as the Son of God, Lord, Peacemaker, Saviour of the World and Coming King – and many other things besides. The devil is constantly firing salvos of flaming arrows at us – arrows of persecution, temptation, deception, oppression, victimization, marginalization, and so on. These arrows are designed to immobilise us and render us inactive and unproductive in the spiritual battle. But we can counter them. God's armour is upon us and this armour includes an extremely effective shield, especially when we stand together in as freedom fighters.

In Paul's day, the first Christians lived in a culture where the Emperors were deified and where the world was being brought into one order under his rule. Today it seems that there is more and more talk of a new world order and more and more images of Empire around us. Indeed, some are even warning about the re-emergence of the Roman Empire in a rebooted form in our own times. In such a context, freedom fighters are more and more going to be called to make a stand for true faith in Christ, especially as the spirit of anti-Christ increases its activity in hostile, secularised social structures.

Freedom fighters will need to call out to each other, 'shields up!'

This highlights the second way in which we must understand the word "faith". Faith doesn't just refer to believing the right things. It refers to behaving in the right way. In a world where nation states are losing their sovereignty and countries are being harnessed into a new world order there are signs that Christians are increasingly being forced to choose between submission to social and demonic powers and loyalty or faithfulness to Jesus Christ. As freedom fighters, will you fight with the spiritual weapons at your disposal for the freedom that Christ won for you? Will you not only raise your shield and defend THE faith (which is faith in Christ), but will you also raise your shields and proclaim, "I will defend my right to be faithful to my Lord and Saviour Jesus Christ, even to the point of death."

I have a feeling that we are going to have to get a whole lot more radical in the future - not just in the matter of believing the right things about Jesus (and decreeing them), but also in behaving in a way that Jesus wants us to behave.

Which will you choose when the ignited arrows start falling from the sky?

CHAPTER 7 | LIFTING YOUR SHIELD

Will you surrender to the powers or will you raise your shield and say, "Jesus is Lord and there is no other!"

To illustrate the importance of the freedom fighter's choices, let me finish with a story.

In the winter of AD 320, Lucinius ordered all Roman soldiers to renounce Christianity and to offer a sacrifice to the Roman gods. His edict reached the Thundering Legion at Sabaste and the order was duly passed down to the legionaries.

Forty Christians in the legion withstood threats, beatings, and torture and refused to obey the edict, choosing instead to obey a higher authority. They declared, 'You shall have no other gods before me. You shall not make for yourself an idol, whether in the form of anything that is in heaven above, or that is on the earth beneath, or that is in the water under the earth. You shall not bow down to them or worship them.' In retaliation, the legion marched the men to a frozen lake where they were ordered to remove their armour and clothing and stand naked, as a form of slow execution, on a frozen lake.

The legionaries lit a large fire on the shore with a warm bath and food to tempt the Christians to make the pagan sacrifice, renounce their Christian faith, and save their lives. The commander told them, 'You may come ashore when you are ready to deny your faith.' But the men began to pray, 'O Lord, forty wrestlers have come forth to fight for Thee. Grant that forty wrestlers may gain the victory!'

The mother of the youngest legionary was present. She called out to him from the shore, where the warm fire and hot bath was beckoning, and enticed her son to abandon the others. However, there was a centurion on the bank called Sempronius. He watched as the remaining Christian legionaries continued to cry out, 'Grant that forty wrestlers may gain the victory!' In response to this extraordinary bravery, Centurion Sempronius confessed Jesus as Christ, removed his armour, weapons and clothing, walked across the ice and joined the thirty nine Christian soldiers on the lake. The next morning the forty martyrs of Sabaste (as they came to be known) were found dead on the ice and their faithful resistance to the dark and oppressive powers of their day has been recorded for all time in the annals of history.

As freedom fighters, choose today whom you will serve!

Choose the one who set you free.

Get free and stay free.

And by faith, bring that freedom to the world.

CHAPTER 7 | LIFTING YOUR SHIELD

APPLYING THE FREEDOM FIGHTING PRINCIPLES

What am I going to *do* in response to what I've read in this chapter?

Action Point 1

Action Point 2

Action Point 3

What am I going to pray for as a result of what I've read?

Prayer Point 1

Prayer Point 2

Prayer Point 3

PERSONAL TRAINING:

Spend some time considering the questions in the box and bring these to the Lord in prayer.

> **The Apostle Peter encouraged us to set Jesus apart as Lord in our hearts (1 Peter 3:15). This means a daily honouring of the uniqueness and supremacy of Jesus Christ in our devotions. Spend some time in your secret place declaring by faith that Jesus is the following:**
>
> - Son of God
> - Lord of All
> - Prince of Peace
> - Saviour of the World
> - Coming King
>
> **When you have declared each of these by faith, turn each truth into worship and watch as your vision of Jesus increases every day**

CHAPTER 7 | LIFTING YOUR SHIELD

GROUP TRAINING:

Spend time as group proclaiming that Jesus is the following:

- Son of God
- Lord of All
- Prince of Peace
- Saviour of the World
- Coming King

Turn these decrees into worship, giving Jesus the highest praise

Vow together to be faithful to Jesus until death (Revelation 2:10)

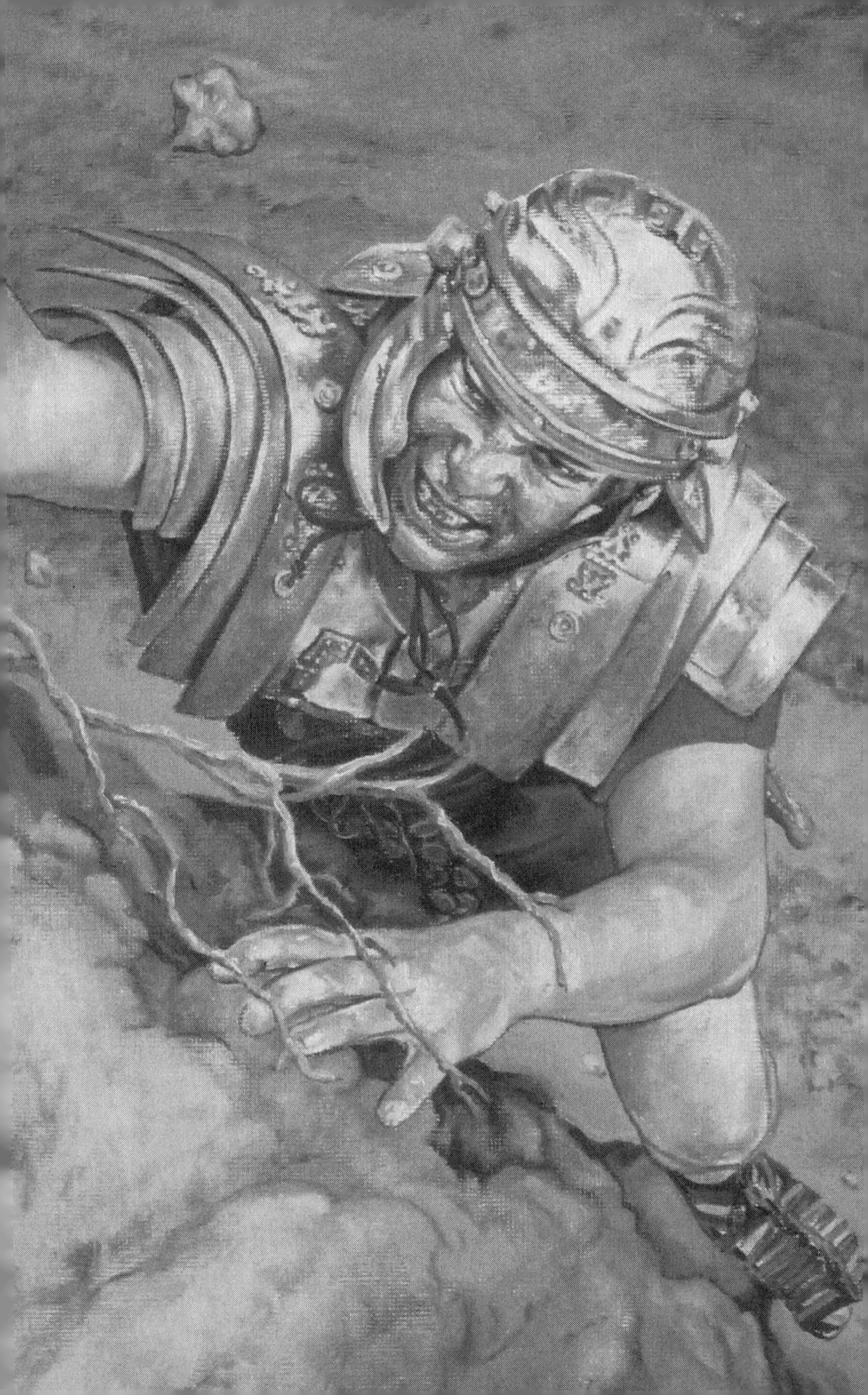

CHAPTER 8

PROTECTING YOUR MIND

How much attention do you give on a day-to-day basis to what you're thinking? Do you guard your mind by ensuring that your thinking is in alignment to what the Father says in his Book, the Bible? Or do you allow your thoughts to be affected and infected by the philosophies and attitudes of contemporary culture? Is your mind conformed to the Word or to the world? To quote Hamlet, "that is the question."

If you and I are to be effective freedom fighters, then we must make sure that in our minds we get free and stay free from every deception born of the world, the flesh and the devil. The battle is so often fought in the mind. How we think determines what we do in life. Put another way, what we believe radically influences how we behave. "As a man thinketh in his heart, so is he" (Proverbs 23:7, KJV). If our thoughts are bound by the enemy's lies then we are not free people. If we are not free people we are not going to set people free.

It stands to reason then that we should daily give attention to our thought life, making sure that our minds are renewed by the truth of the Word and the Spirit, taking any thought captive that has been sent by the enemy to restrict our sense of who we are in Christ and what we are on this earth to do - to bring freedom to the captives.

The most ferocious and significant battlefields of this world are therefore not in some faraway place like Iraq or Syria but closer than our hands and feet. They are between our ears. That is where the most important battles are fought and won, in our minds.

Receiving from Jesus

It should come as no surprise then that the Apostle Paul talks about a new piece of armour for the freedom fighter, one specifically designed to protect our minds. I am referring of course to the helmet of salvation. Here is the NKJV of Ephesians 6:14-17:

Stand therefore, having girded your waist with truth, having put on the breastplate of righteousness, and having shod your feet with the preparation of the gospel of peace; above all, taking the shield of faith with which you will be able to quench all the fiery darts of the wicked one. And take the helmet of salvation.

What did Paul have in mind when he spoke of this helmet? He was thinking of the Roman legionary again. The Roman soldier's helmet was made of bronze and was essentially an oval bowl weighing 4-5 lbs with a rear peak which jutted out at the nape of the neck. This was sometimes designed with small ridges or steps which acted to break the force of downward blows, deflecting them onto the neck guards. At the sides of the helmet there were metal flanges or cheek guards to protect the face and throat. These hung down to the neck line and had holes for the ears to allow the legionary to hear orders in battle. These cheek pieces, along with the oval bowl of the helmet itself, were lined with woollen felt to absorb blows and increase comfort. All in all, the legionary's helmet was a superbly designed item of armour.

When Paul tells us to take up our helmets, this is what he imagined. Notice the difference in language here. Up until now, Paul has been telling us to put on the belt of truth, the shoes of peace and the shield of faith. Now he instructs us to receive the helmet of salvation; this is the sense of the verb "take" here. Paul is using an imperative; in other words, he is issuing a command. "Accept this piece of armour," he says. We should imagine Jesus, far greater than any emperor, presenting us with a resplendent battle helmet, carefully designed to protect our minds from the lies of the enemy. This helmet had the same function in relation to the mind as the breastplate had in relation to the heart. Indeed, if the breastplate is the Christian's heart-protector, the helmet is the Christian's mind-protector. That is some picture!

From Slavery to Sonship

Paul tells us that this helmet is to do with "salvation." What did Paul mean by "salvation"? And why is it important for the freedom fighter to think correctly about this subject? To answer these questions let's look at what Paul says about salvation in the rest of Ephesians. In chapter 2 he begins by stressing what we have been saved from. He writes:

And you He made alive, who were dead in trespasses and sins, in which you once walked according to the course of this world, according to the prince of the power of the air, the spirit who now works in the sons of disobedience, among whom also we all once conducted ourselves in the lusts of our flesh, fulfilling the desires of the flesh and of the mind, and were by nature children of wrath, just as the others.

Here Paul shows us that before we were saved we were slaves. We were slaves to a life of trespasses and sins, a life ruled by the devil, a life that made us sons of disobedience, a life that was surrendered to the lusts of the flesh, a life that meant that we were children of wrath - people who deserved divine judgment not mercy.

Having told us the bad news, Paul now turns to the good news, marking the transition with the simple words 'but God':

But God, who is rich in mercy, because of His great love with which He loved us, even when we were dead in trespasses, made us alive together with Christ (by grace you have been saved), and raised us up together, and made us sit together in the heavenly places in Christ Jesus, that in the ages to come He might show the exceeding riches of His grace in His kindness toward us in Christ Jesus. For by grace you have been saved through faith, and that not of yourselves; it is the gift of God, not of works, lest anyone should boast.

Paul makes it very clear that we could not rescue ourselves from this dark and desperate plight by our own efforts. It was God himself who initiated the rescue plan and he did this because of His rich love, His great mercy and His amazing grace "in Christ Jesus." By sending His only Son into the world to deal with our sins, God demonstrated the extreme lengths to which He was prepared to go to liberate us from our slavery to sin. All that a person needs to do to receive freedom is to accept that it is only by God's grace that we are saved and then choose to enter into a relationship with Christ. When we do that, we are no longer slaves but sons. We are, in fact, royal sons because we find ourselves "seated with Him in the heavenly realms"!

Hallelujah!

All this shows that we are not just delivered *from* something; we are delivered *to* something. God's grace saves us *from* slavery to sin and it also saves us *to* a life of honoured sonship. That is amazing grace indeed!

To underline this, let's remember the beginning of Ephesians where Paul embarks on a long and breathless eulogy of all that God has done for us in Christ. Using a Jewish form of prayer known as the *berakah* (a prayer of thanksgiving), Paul eloquently thanks Abba Father for the fact that we are chosen and adopted:

Blessed be the God and Father of our Lord Jesus Christ, who has blessed us with every spiritual blessing in the heavenly places in Christ, just as He chose us in Him before the foundation of the world, that we should be holy and without blame before Him in love, having predestined us to adoption as sons by Jesus Christ to Himself, according to the good pleasure of His will, to the praise of the glory of His grace, by which He has made us accepted in the Beloved.

Notice here the reference to being 'predestined to adoption.' As we saw in chapter 2, in the Roman practice of adoption a slave's son was set free from a desperate and dangerous life by being purchased out of slavery. This act was performed by an adopting father whose generosity to the child was unbounded. Once he was adopted the boy's previous debts were all cancelled and he was given the unearned privilege of a new father, a new freedom, a new family, and indeed a new fortune.

Applying this to the life of the Christian, Paul says that we too have been bought out of slavery. Our freedom from sin has not been purchased with gold or silver but rather with the blood of the Son of God.

Seen in this light, salvation is a glorious transition from slavery to sonship. Thanks to the extreme measures taken by the One and Only Son by nature, we can be set free from our slavery to sin and become the royal, adopted sons and daughters of the King of Heaven.

This is a priceless privilege!

Thinking like a Son

Freedom fighters know that there is a fierce spiritual war raging in the cosmos. The enemy is fighting hard to keep unsaved people in a state of slavery and he is fighting equally vigorously to ensnare those who are saved and to turn them into P.O.Ws, prisoners of war. Freedom fighters are committed to setting the captives free. They are wholly devoted to the cause of bringing God's freedom to those enslaved by the devil. To do this, we have to keep making sure that we are not dragged back into the condition of slavery from which we have been so glorious rescued. We have to protect our minds and guard our thinking so that we do not become deceived. Once we are deceived we become bound and once we are bound we can no longer set the captives free because we ourselves are in captivity.

For a freedom fighter to stand firm against the brutal onslaughts of the enemy, the helmet of salvation is an absolute prerequisite. The freedom fighter needs to have his mind protected by the great truth that we have received salvation *from* sin and *unto* sonship. Half measures here are not enough. It is not sufficient to know that we have been saved from the shame of a sinful life. We must also know that we have been saved *to* the honour of being an adopted son of God. Those who know such things in their redeemed and renewed minds live in a perpetual state of assurance that they are forgiven and indeed 'accepted in the Beloved.' Nothing can persuade them otherwise. Whatever the wicked one may throw at them, they stand securely in their honoured position in Christ.

This is why the mind is so important. The mind is where the evil one seeks to attack us most violently because he knows that the way a person thinks determines everything. If the evil one can make me think like a slave again, then I will behave like a slave again but if I intentionally guard my mind against such deception, then I can daily stand my ground and declare, "I am a royal son of heaven by adoption and no strategy from the pit of hell or from the thoughts of men can ever remove that honour from my life."

It is here that we catch the urgency of Paul's command to receive the helmet of salvation. Salvation is something we receive. As Paul is at pains to emphasize in Ephesians 2, we are saved not by our own efforts, lest any of us should boast, but as a result of the grace of God displayed in the sacrificial death of His Son. Those who choose to put their faith and trust in the finished work of the Cross are saved. They do not earn their salvation. They receive it

CHAPTER 8 | PROTECTING YOUR MIND

freely as a result of repentance from sin and faith in Christ.

Notice I said "repentance". The Greek word translated repentance is *metanoia*. That is a combination of two words, one meaning "change" and the other meaning "mind". To repent is to change your thinking. It is to stop believing one thing and to start believing quite another. It means no longer thinking like a slave but thinking like a son.

Only amazing grace could bring about such a radical transformation.

That is truly a change of mind.

It is, in fact, a complete paradigm shift.

Receiving Your Inheritance

Protecting the mind is vital if we are to remain free and indeed if we are to bring freedom to others. This is why Paul talks about the importance of the mind a number of times in Ephesians. In Ephesians 2.3 he speaks about how we fulfilled the desires of our minds before we were Christians. The word translated "mind" here is *dianoia*, meaning "mind, imagination, or understanding". Paul uses the same word in Ephesians 4.13 when he describes how our understanding was darkened prior to our salvation. Now that we are in Christ, the eyes of our dianoia, our understanding, can be enlightened (Ephesians 1.18). Our thought life can be flooded with the light of God's truth. Our imaginations can be on fire with the love of God! That is a profound transformation indeed. It is a transfiguration of the mind!

Perhaps the most detailed description of the mind-transforming implications of salvation is found in Ephesians 4:17-24:

This I say, therefore, and testify in the Lord, that you should no longer walk as the rest of the Gentiles walk, <u>in the futility of their mind, having their understanding darkened</u>, being alienated from *the life of God, because of the ignorance that is in them, because of the hardening of their heart; who, being past feeling, have given themselves over to lewdness, to work all uncleanness with greediness. But you have not so learned Christ, if indeed you have heard Him and have been taught by Him, as the truth is in Jesus: that you put off, concerning your former conduct, the old man which grows corrupt according to the deceitful lusts, <u>and be renewed in the spirit of your mind</u>, and that you put on the new man which was created according to God, in true righteousness and holiness.*

There is no greater or more graphic description of the battle for the mind in the entire Bible! This battle for the human mind was fierce enough before we were in Christ but Paul makes it clear that it is just as ferocious if not more so now that we are in Christ. In Christ, we need to put on the helmet of salvation and recognize the full glory of our identity in the Beloved. In union with the Son by nature, we who are adopted sons and daughters not only put sin to death, we also experience the dynamic power of the resurrection. More glorious still, in Christ, we are elevated above the dark powers of the cosmos and are seated in the heavenly realms, empowered to live the ascended life. We are royal, adopted sons seated with the Son by nature!

This is the full inheritance of our adoption as sons and it is an inheritance that is only accessed by revelation. This is why Paul is so eager for his readers to know these truths and why he prays so earnestly for their minds to be spiritually illuminated. Look at his prayer in Ephesians 1:18-21, a prayer that

the eyes of your understanding being enlightened; that you may know what is the hope of His calling, what are the riches of the glory of His inheritance in the saints, and what is the exceeding greatness of His power toward us who believe, according to the working of His mighty power which He worked in Christ when He raised Him from the dead and seated Him at His right hand in the heavenly places, far

CHAPTER 8 | PROTECTING YOUR MIND

above all principality and power and might and dominion, and every name that is named, not only in this age but also in that which is to come.

Why is Paul so passionate that believers should understand such things? It is because he knows from his own experience that a person who understands who he really is also appreciates what he really has. Put another way, the greater our understanding of our position in Christ, the greater our exercise of authority in Christ will be.

Putting on the helmet of salvation is therefore an essential daily discipline. Standing up in our belt and breastplate, wearing our shoes and carrying our shield, we remind ourselves – we RE-MIND ourselves – of our position in Christ. As freedom fighters, we learn to declare these great truths about who we are and what we have in Christ:

'I am no longer a slave to sin but a son. My old sinful life has been crucified in the death of Christ. I now live and operate in the same power that raised Christ Jesus from the dead. More than that, I am seated with the Ascended Lord in the heavenly realms. In him, I am more than an overcomer and victorious over every assault of the enemy. Thanks to what the Word of God teaches, I am fully persuaded that I am forgiven, accepted, and redeemed. Thanks to the work of the Holy Spirit in my life, I know by experience that I am beloved, chosen, adopted and special. I am honoured not ashamed. I am saved from slavery and I now enjoy the status of a son. Therefore I shall never be separated from the Father's love. These things are sealed upon my heart and inscribed upon my mind, which is being renewed in the Holy Spirit and protected by the helmet of salvation every day of my life.'

The Call to Sonship

What would happen on the earth if every Christian man were

to wake up today, put on the belt of truth and the breastplate of righteousness, the shoes of readiness and the shield of faith, and receive again by revelation – through the Word and the Spirit – the wonderful truth that they are saved from slavery to sonship? Such men without doubt would have the capacity to stand firm in the battle and advance the Gospel of peace in the world. Such men would not doubt either their identity or their authority. They would know who they are in Christ and they would use what they have in Christ. They would appreciate their royal position and they would operate in their royal power and authority. In short, their minds would be transformed and their thinking sanctified.

How vital is the helmet of salvation!

How important it is to think daily like a saved son!

I once heard a speaker use an illustration which explains what this looks like.

"Recently I got married," he said. "My wife works in the evenings at a local restaurant so I have to make my own meals those evenings. Sometimes, instead of cooking for myself, I go round to my dad's house. He lives in the same town. I have a key to the front door. I just let myself in, go to the kitchen, fetch some leftovers from the fridge, heat them up, sit down on my dad's sofa, switch on my dad's TV and eat my dad's food."

He then paused before explaining the illustration.

"The reason I can do this is because I am a son not a servant. Had I been the window cleaner, let's say, I would have made an appointment. I would have knocked on the door and been allowed access to the rooms, yes, but I would not have been allowed to raid the fridge or watch TV because his job is to serve my dad."

Finally, he made the application.

"How different this is for me as his son! I do not need to make

CHAPTER 8 | PROTECTING YOUR MIND

an appointment. I have a key. I have access to my father's resources. I don't have to work in my father's house. All I have to do is enter and rest."

When you start to think like that, you have truly put on the helmet of salvation!

For a man to be a true freedom fighter, this piece of armour must therefore never be neglected and must forever be protected. When a man places this helmet on his head, he reminds himself that he is saved *from* the shame of sin and saved *to* the honour of being a son. In the process, something dynamic and dramatic takes place in his mind, understanding and imagination. He starts to see himself differently – as a son of the Most High God.

He is no longer a pauper; he is a prince.

He is no longer abandoned; he is adopted.

He is no longer humiliated; he is honoured.

He is no longer a nobody; he is a somebody.

He is no longer ordinary; he is extraordinary.

He is no longer powerless; he is powerful.

He is no longer a slave; he is a son.

Freedom fighters have a mandate to place the helmet of salvation on their heads and to remember daily who they truly are in Christ.

Never forget: you are defined by your position, not by your performance. Saved by grace alone through faith alone in Christ alone, you stand firm in the fight and you win your skirmishes in the epic struggle against dark powers. You always listen for the Father's voice while your sword beats against your shield – a voice that cries out from a torn heaven, "You are my beloved son!" Your helmet may be dented and battered in the battle, but you hold your head high and your plumed feathers tremble marvellously in the wind of the Spirit. In tight ranks with other such men, you occupy enemy territory and you bring the peace of Christ to the earth.

You are part of a band of brothers.

You are a freedom fighter for the Father.

CHAPTER 8 | PROTECTING YOUR MIND

APPLYING THE FREEDOM FIGHTING PRINCIPLES

What am I going to *do* in response to what I've read in this chapter?

Action Point 1

___

Action Point 2

___

Action Point 3

___

What am I going to pray for as a result of what I've read?

Prayer Point 1

___

Prayer Point 2

___

Prayer Point 3

___

PERSONAL TRAINING:

Spend some time considering the questions in the box and bring these to the Lord in prayer.

> **Imagine yourself receiving the helmet of salvation from Jesus. Make the following statement your decree on a regular basis in your private devotions:**
>
> 'I am no longer a slave to sin but a son. My old sinful life has been crucified in the death of Christ. I now live and operate in the same power that raised Christ Jesus from the dead. More than that, I am seated with the Ascended Lord in the heavenly realms. In him, I am more than an overcomer and victorious over every assault of the enemy. Thanks to what the Word of God teaches, I am fully persuaded that I am forgiven, accepted, and redeemed. Thanks to the work of the Holy Spirit in my life, I know by experience that I am beloved, chosen, adopted and special. I am honoured not ashamed. I am saved from slavery and I now enjoy the status of a son. Therefore I shall never be separated from the Father's love. These things are sealed upon my heart and inscribed upon my mind, which is being renewed in the Holy Spirit and protected by the helmet of salvation every day of my life.'
>
> **Allow the Holy Spirit to make these words real in your mind and heart**
>
> **Ask Him to wash away any thoughts contrary to these truths**
>
> **Renounce any lies of the enemy that contradict these truths, in the name of Jesus**

CHAPTER 8 | PROTECTING YOUR MIND

GROUP TRAINING:

Stand as a group of men and thank your Heavenly Father that when you decree a matter, it is established (Job 22:28)

Now take hold of your royal authority as an adopted son of God and make the following statement your collective decree:

'I am no longer a slave to sin but a son. My old sinful life has been crucified in the death of Christ. I now live and operate in the same power that raised Christ Jesus from the dead. More than that, I am seated with the Ascended Lord in the heavenly realms. In him, I am more than an overcomer and victorious over every assault of the enemy. Thanks to what the Word of God teaches, I am fully persuaded that I am forgiven, accepted, and redeemed. Thanks to the work of the Holy Spirit in my life, I know by experience that I am beloved, chosen, adopted and special. I am honoured not ashamed. I am saved from slavery and I now enjoy the status of a son. Therefore I shall never be separated from the Father's love. These things are sealed upon my heart and inscribed upon my mind, which is being renewed in the Holy Spirit and protected by the helmet of salvation every day of my life.'

If any member of your *contubernium* is feeling distressed or depressed in their minds, gather round them and pray in faith for freedom

Renounce the lies of the enemy and welcome the Spirit of truth

Make a group agreement to have your minds conformed to the Word and not the world

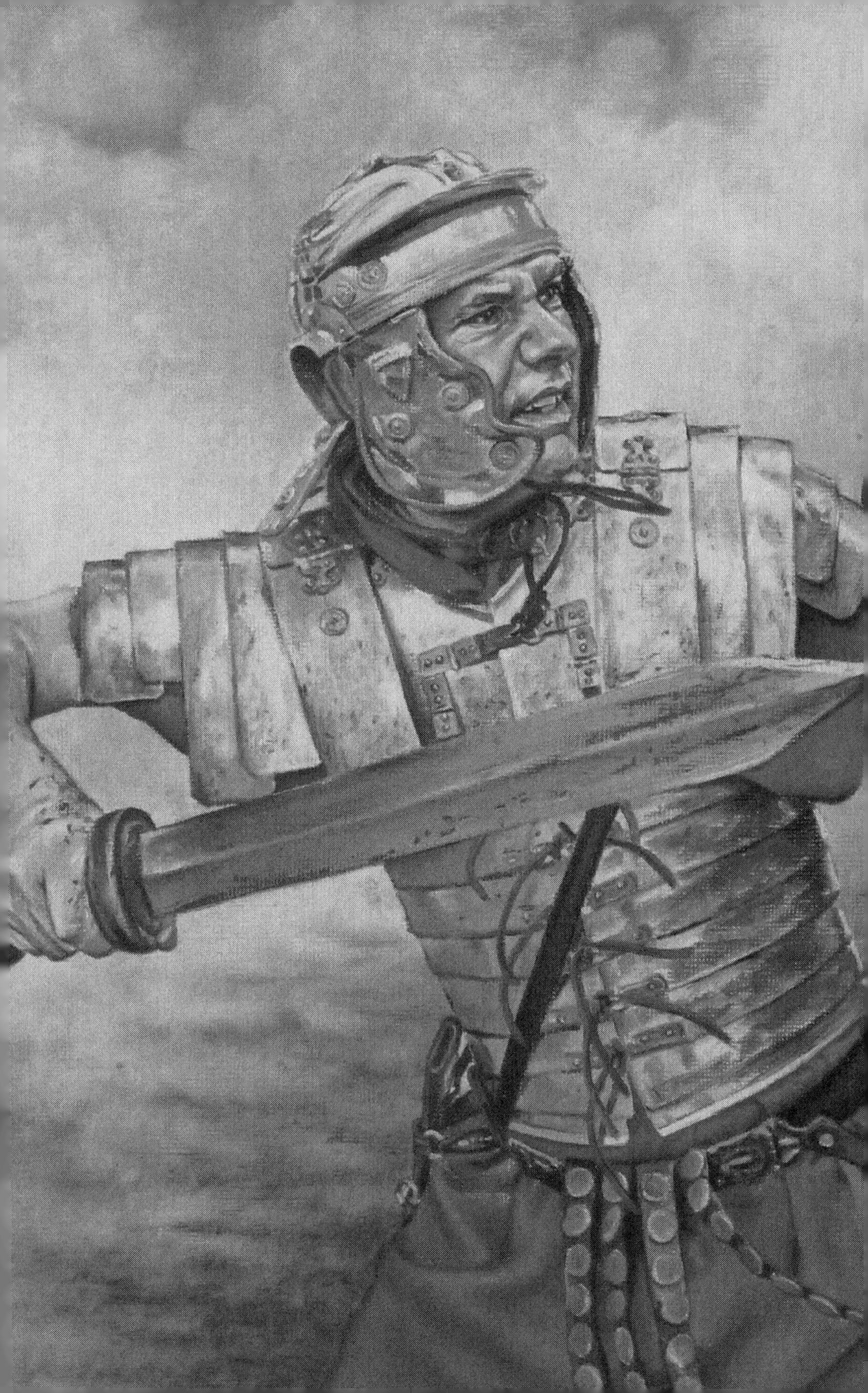

CHAPTER 9

DRAWING YOUR SWORD

What was Jesus' defence against the devil during the forty nights and days of temptation in the desert? In a word, it was the *Word*. Jesus found his freedom from enemy attack by doing two things: firstly, remembering the words of Scripture that he had learned, even as a boy; secondly, declaring these Scriptures as absolute truth, with faith and confidence in the power of God's Word to send the devil on his way.

Let's look at the passage in Matthew 4:

Then Jesus was led up by the Spirit into the wilderness to be tempted by the devil. And when He had fasted forty days and forty nights, afterward He was hungry. Now when the tempter came to Him, he said, "If You are the Son of God, command that these stones become bread."

But He answered and said, <u>"It is written, 'Man shall not live by bread alone, but by every word that proceeds from the mouth of God.'"</u>

Then the devil took Him up into the holy city, set Him on the pinnacle of the temple, and said to Him, "If You are the Son of God, throw Yourself down. For it is written:

'He shall give His angels charge over you,'

and,

'In their hands they shall bear you up,

Lest you dash your foot against a stone.'"

Jesus said to him, "It <u>is written again, 'You shall not tempt the LORD your God.'</u>"

Again, the devil took Him up on an exceedingly high mountain, and showed Him all the kingdoms of the world and their glory. And he said to Him, "All these things I will give You if You will fall down and worship me."

Then Jesus said to him, "Away with you, Satan! For <u>it is written, 'You shall worship the LORD your God, and Him only you shall serve.'</u>"

Then the devil left Him, and behold, angels came and ministered to Him.

What a lasting lesson this is!

We are all sons of the Father by adoption. We are also soldiers in the Father's army - Dad's Army, if you will. We are ordinary people with an extraordinary capacity. This capacity is at least in part due to the fact that we have a weapon at our disposal that has the authority to demolish strongholds and to break the power of every assault of the enemy.

That weapon is the Word of God, the Bible and no man can be an effective freedom fighter without memorising it and proclaiming it.

This is why the Apostle Paul now moves on to the final piece of armour in the Roman soldier's panoply - the sword.

Slaying the Serpent

After encouraging his readers to receive the helmet of salvation, Paul now tells them to receive from God "the sword of the Spirit."

When Paul mentions this sword, he clearly has in mind the *gladius* of the Roman legionary. This was neither a long slashing sword nor a short stabbing sword. In the time of the Emperor Augustus the regulation sword was between 40-56 centimetres long and it was eight centimetres wide across the shoulders. It

CHAPTER 9 | DRAWING YOUR SWORD

had a wasp-waisted blade and a long tapering point. It weighed between 1.2 and 1.6 kilograms and was sheathed inside a tinned or silvered scabbard embossed with motifs celebrating Augustus' reign. Such swords were attached to the legionary's belt using a four ring suspension system. Senior officers and centurions wore their swords on the left of their body. The soldiers wore theirs on the right.

The legionary kept this weapon at his side at all times. He had regular training in swordsmanship and kept his blade clean and sharp. This weapon, designed for the cut and thrust of close quarter fighting, was usually employed after soldiers had hurled their spears at the enemy. Having caused death and confusion by a volley of missiles, the legionaries would charge into the ranks of dazed and dying enemy soldiers and finish them off with the sword. The sword was accordingly an offensive weapon.

With this in mind, let's look carefully at what Paul says.

First of all, we should pause and reflect on the metaphor of the sword itself. While Paul most likely has one eye on the Roman *gladius* he may also be thinking of the Old Testament picture of God as the Warrior. Look at Isaiah 27.1:

In that day the LORD with His severe sword, great and strong, will punish Leviathan the fleeing serpent, Leviathan that twisted serpent; and He will slay the reptile that is in the sea.

Notice the victim of God's sword. Leviathan is the creature that is stabbed by the Divine Warrior. Leviathan is a Biblical symbol for the devil (Job 41.1-11; Psalm 72.12-14; Isaiah 51.9; Ezekiel 29.3; Ezekiel 32.2; Revelation 12.3-4). God uses his severe sword to punish the twisted, ancient serpent that has caused His people untold harm since the beginning of time in the Garden of Eden. It is therefore not people whom God stabs; it is the *power* oppressing them. This underlines Paul's point that we fight against principalities and powers not flesh and blood. The metaphor of the sword is therefore not intended to fuel aggression towards human beings, however cruel they may be. It is a spiritual weapon to be used in our corporate stand against the dark powers that influence those people.

The second thing to note is that Paul calls this sword 'the sword of the Spirit.' This does not mean that the sword comes from the Spirit of God. It means that the sword is made effective by the Spirit of God. It is the Holy Spirit who enables us to do damage to the enemy's ranks because it is the Spirit who makes the sword such a devastating, penetrating weapon against evil. With the sword, freedom fighters can pierce the darkness.

The third thing we should understand is that Paul's phraseology is slightly different in relation to the sword from the other armour items. Let's remind ourselves of his description of the other pieces:

The belt of truth

The breastplate of righteousness

The shoes of the readiness of the gospel of peace

The shield of faith

The helmet of salvation

In each of these five descriptions the former represents the latter. In other words, the belt represents truth; the breastplate represents righteousness, and so on. Not so in the case of the sword. The sword does not represent the Spirit. Rather, the sword – which is 'of the Spirit' - represents the 'word of God.' Paul is not saying that the sword is the Spirit because we cannot wield the Spirit. The Holy Spirit is beyond all forms of human manipulation. He is the unlimited and untameable power of the living God.

Application and Declaration

If the sword represents 'the word of God', then what did Paul mean by this?

Here we need to make a distinction between what the "word

CHAPTER 9 | DRAWING YOUR SWORD

of God" meant to Christians at the time in which Ephesians was written and what the "Word of God" (capitalised) means to Christians today.

In the time of the Apostle Paul, the New Testament was in the process of being written. Indeed, this letter - the Letter to the Ephesians - is one of the books that would later be acknowledged as part of the New Testament.

Paul was therefore writing before what we know as the Bible was formed.

The full Bible, Old and New Testaments, was still in formation and it would be several hundred years before the fathers of the church (Bishops and theologians) would agree what the sixty six books of the Bible were.

So we need to take care. At the time, Paul did not mean the Bible in our sense of the word. However, he would be entirely happy with the common interpretation today that the "word of God" in Ephesians 6 means the "Word of God", the Bible. I am entirely convinced that the Apostle Paul would agree with those who say that today the sword of God's Word is a reference to the sacred, incisive and authoritative text we know as Holy Scripture. As we saw in Matthew 4, the Son of God used Scripture as a sword!

If it was good enough for the Son by nature, then it's certainly good enough for those of us who are sons by adoption.

We need to go beyond this, however.

We can learn from the Son as we seek to be good sons and say this: that using the sword of the Spirit which is the "word of God" is the powerful application of Bible truths in a given situation, especially situations of conflict. When a freedom fighter wields the sword of the Spirit, he brings out of his memory bank a Scripture passage that is perfectly tailored to the moment and the need in question. The declaration of this word then brings peace where there has been hostility, clarity where there has been confusion, welfare where there has been warfare, and liberation where there has been oppression.

Wielding the sword is therefore something very specific.

It is the incisive application and declaration of the written Word of God.

It is the written Word spoken out.

The Solution to Dilution

Why do we need this weapon?

Let's keep our minds focused on what Paul teaches in Ephesians 6 which is this: that as freedom fighters we are engaged in spiritual warfare. Our battle is not against people but against demonic principalities and powers (Leviathan, the twisted serpent) and our battle strategies therefore have to be carefully orchestrated to meet the enemy's wicked tactics. What are these tactics? In chapter 3, 'Knowing your Enemy,' I identified seven major battle plans that the enemy uses in Scripture and which we have seen him use throughout history, including in our own lives. These seven strategies are:

1. Deception - getting us to believe lies
2. Depravity - getting us to indulge the flesh
3. Division - getting us to fall out with others
4. Doubt - getting us to question what we believe
5. Depression - getting us to feel despondent
6. Dilution - getting us to water down the Gospel
7. Distraction - getting us to focus on problems

In chapter 3 I showed how each of the pieces in the freedom fighter's armour is specifically designed to combat and conquer each of these insidious assaults.

CHAPTER 9 | DRAWING YOUR SWORD

The belt of truth defends us against deception.

The breastplate of righteousness defends us against depravity.

The shoes of the Gospel of peace defend us against division.

The shield of faith batters and beats the enemy's attempts to get us to doubt God.

The helmet of salvation combats depression.

The sword of the Spirit, the Word of God, defends us against dilution. When we daily walk in God's Word, we keep our thinking in alignment with the mind of Christ rather than with the thinking of this world. Freedom fighters whose minds and hearts are constantly steeped in the Word of God therefore have an armoury of Scriptures in their memory banks. When people try to dilute the Gospel or distort the Scriptures, freedom fighters will be able to locate and deploy the perfect Scriptural passages to confront and conquer this liberalizing and revisionist spirit. With the powerful assistance of the Holy Spirit, the application and declaration of these Scriptures proves to be incisive. As the writer to the Hebrews puts it,

The word of God is living and powerful, and sharper than any two-edged sword, piercing even to the division of soul and spirit, and of joints and marrow, and is a discerner of the thoughts and intents of the heart.

When we raise the sword of the Spirit, the principalities and powers which lie behind atheistic and even anti-theistic opinions are confronted. These powers have already been judged at the Cross. As Paul says in Colossians 2.15: "having disarmed principalities and powers, He made a public spectacle of them, triumphing over them in it" (i.e. in his death on the Cross). These powers are already defeated but every time the sword is raised and the Word of God declared, these sinister powers feel the penetrating thrust of the sword of the Spirit.

One day, of course, they will be terminated by the sharp two-edged sword of Christ's mouth forever (Revelation 1.16; 2.12).

In the meantime, the enemy's attempts to dilute God's truth are stopped in their tracks by freedom fighters with raised swords.

Speaking in Love

Freedom fighters need to understand that wielding the sword is not the calling of the preacher alone but the calling of every man in Christ. When Paul tells his readers to put on the armour pieces, he is not talking to preachers but to everyone. He uses "you" plural in Ephesians 6. "All of you take up the sword." It is simply no good then for freedom fighters to say that reading and preaching the Word of God is the sole responsibility of the evangelist or the pastor. It is a mandate for every man in Christ. All of us need to learn to take our swords from their scabbards, raise it with other men, and thrust its penetrating blade into those powers that keep people in enmity when they could be living in harmony with God and each other.

This means that the freedom fighter must be prepared to bring out their swords whenever it is needed. They cannot just go to church once a week and settle for seeing someone else wield their spiritual sword in the pulpit. Their own swords must be brought out and used on a daily basis. And they need to be used in close quarter interaction with people whose minds have been darkened by the powers of this age.

Here we need to remember that the legionary's sword was originally intended for close combat. If Paul had been thinking of long distance warfare he would have said, "Take up the spear of the Spirit, which is the word of God." But he was not. He was thinking of direct communication with people who are under the influence of hostile powers. He was probably envisaging face-to-face dialogue in which the man of war – at enmity with God and others – is disarmed by the incisive power of the freedom fighter bearing the Gospel of peace.

In all of this, the freedom fighter must remember that the sword

CHAPTER 9 | DRAWING YOUR SWORD

is a sword of truth and truth needs to be handled with humility and honour, not with pride and disdain. There are too many Christians on the earth raising the sword in the wrong way at the moment, conducting witch hunts in the church and the world, chastising and denigrating both believers and unbelievers for taking a different theological or political position from their own. There are too many, in other words, who behave as if they are the only ones who know the truth.

This is pride.

And pride comes before a fall.

The true freedom fighter realises full well that the sword of the Spirit, the word of God, is God's written and eternal truth but this does not make the freedom fighter arrogant or domineering. Rather, the freedom fighter always holds in high regard the value that Paul teaches two chapters before Ephesians 6 about "speaking truth in love". Speaking the truth in love builds people up. Speaking the truth with a haughty, know-it-all, dishonouring tone is extremely unloving and tears people down.

As freedom fighters, we know the power that lies in the tongue. We know that words can edify and we know that words can vilify. We therefore seek to engage in the application and declaration of God's truth in the kindest way possible, knowing that it is kindness that leads people to repentance, not sternness (Romans 2:4).

Freedom fighters therefore use the sword with humility and honour.

They speak God's truth with God's love.

They always remember to aim the blade at the power behind the person not the person who is being led astray.

They always hold fast to the fact that other human beings are our friends.

It is Satan who is the enemy.

Reading the Bible

In order to be able to use our swords with maximum impact, we need to be people who are committed to the spiritual discipline of reading the Word of God. In the Roman army, discipline was essential not just in the day-to-day running of the Roman military machine but in the heat of battle. In the army, discipline was absolutely essential. It was the disciplined man who progressed in the ranks and who prevailed in war.

The same is true for freedom fighters. Those who engage in spiritual disciplines such as the personal reading of God's Word, as well as group Bible study in their *conturbernium*, will have a far greater chance of progressing in times of peace and prevailing in times of war. Those who read and revere the Word will prosper.

As you engage in this spiritual discipline, there are four principles always to bear in mind.

The first is to read the Word *regularly*. Those who immerse themselves in the Bible on a consistent basis will grow spiritually. This is a simple fact. Biblical illiteracy leads to spiritual immaturity. Commitment to reading the Word as often as possible brings growth in wisdom and power. No freedom fighter can afford to neglect this discipline.

Furthermore, today we have no excuse. We live at a time when we can download apps onto our smart phones and tablets that are designed to take us through the entire Bible in a year. This means that busy men can read the Word "on the go". They don't have to carve out time. They have to redeem the time they already have!

Read the Word *regularly*.

Secondly, read the Word *responsibly*. You will have noticed from this book how committed I am to understanding what the Bible means in its original context. Never forget the old saying: a text without a context becomes a pretext. When we use Bible verses out of context, we are being irresponsible. We are making the Bible

CHAPTER 9 | DRAWING YOUR SWORD

mean what we want it to mean.

Once again, we have no excuse today. There are apps we can download onto our portable devices that help us to understand what the original authors of the Bible meant in their original situations. Learn to use these. Remember, the dilution and distortion of truth (known as 'heresy') occurs when people don't attend properly to what the Bible originally meant.

Read the Word *responsibly*.

Thirdly, read the Word *respectfully*. There has been a lengthy and vicious, demonic attack on the authority of the Bible, particularly during the twentieth century. The so-called "higher criticism" in Biblical scholarship sought to undermine both the eternal Word of God. It enticed many to ask the serpent's question, "Did God really say?"

The result of this was that instead of using the Bible for the battle, many believers became distracted by the battle for the Bible.

Today it's time to reverse the trend.

As freedom fighters, we are reinstating the Bible for the battle.

We are committed to reading the Bible *respectfully*, sitting under God's Word with humility not standing over it with pride.

Finally, read the Word *relationally*. Too many believers read the Bible religiously - as if it was a rulebook, or a book of laws. But God is not a remote, legal figure in the sky. He is our loving, doting, extravagantly loving, Heavenly Father. He sent Jesus to bring us back into His arms. He sent Jesus to start a relationship, not a religion.

The Bible should therefore be read *relationally*, as a love letter from the perfect Father.

As St Augustine once said, "If the entire Bible was encapsulated in a single sentence, it would cry out like the resounding waves of the sea, 'the Father loves you.'"

Read the Bible as an adoring son not as a religious slave.

Don't intellectualise the Word.

Memorise it.

Then you will be able to wield the sword with the help of the Holy Spirit, engaging in the Spirit-inspired application and declaration of God's truth.

Doing this, freedom fighters will fulfil their calling to set the captives free.

CHAPTER 9 | DRAWING YOUR SWORD

APPLYING THE FREEDOM FIGHTING PRINCIPLES

What am I going to *do* in response to what I've read in this chapter?

Action Point 1

Action Point 2

Action Point 3

What am I going to pray for as a result of what I've read?

Prayer Point 1

Prayer Point 2

Prayer Point 3

PERSONAL TRAINING:

Spend some time considering the questions in the box and bring these to the Lord in prayer.

To what extent do you do the following?

1. Read the Bible Regularly

2: Read the Bible Responsibly

3. Read the Bible Respectfully

4: Read the Bible Relationally

What practical steps are you now going to take in order to engage in the spiritual discipline of Bible study?

Suggestions:

Use Mark Stibbe's 100 Verse Bible and his devotional book, Every Day with the Father (both published by Monarch Books). Also, read and give away copies of his book, God's Word for Every Need (Destiny Image, 2016). Memorize the Bible verses he uses there.

Download and use the app, BiOY - Bible in One Year (Nicky Gumbel). Also, for deeper study, use the Olive Tree Bible study apps suitable for your needs.

CHAPTER 9 | DRAWING YOUR SWORD

GROUP TRAINING:

Discuss the following questions with each other:

What is your current level of discipline as regards reading the Bible?

Do you use any Bible study tools?

What prevents you from reading the Word of God?

What are the harmful effects of neglecting Bible study?

Have you ever regarded the Bible as "the Father's Love Letter" to you?

What difference might it make to do that?

How are you, as a group, going to use the Bible for the battle?

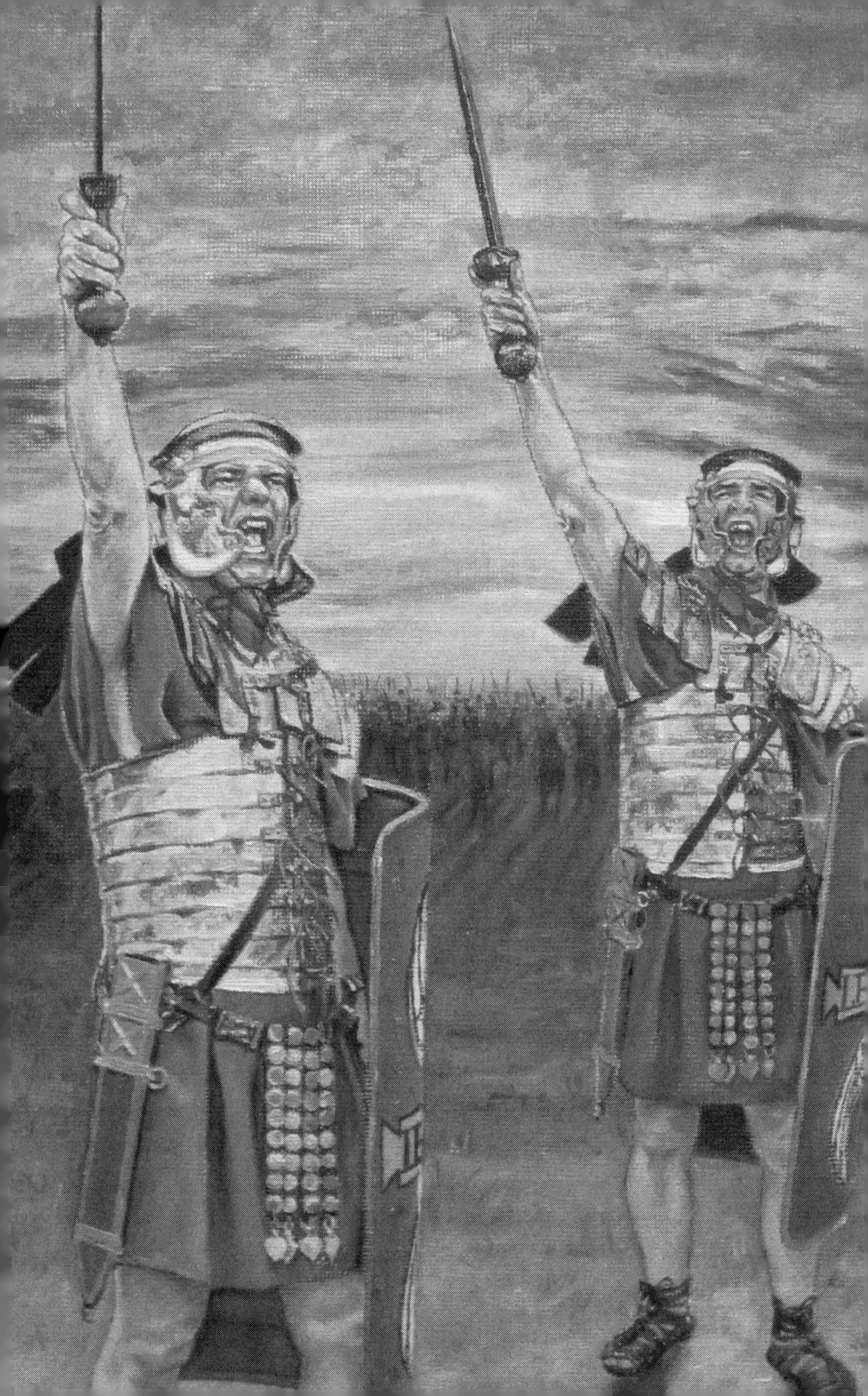

CHAPTER 10

RAISING A LOUD SHOUT

And finally, freedom fighters are men of prayer.

This is why the Apostle Paul finishes off his teaching on the armour of God by telling us to raise the sword of the Spirit (the Word), and in addition

praying always with all prayer and supplication in the Spirit, being watchful to this end with all perseverance and supplication for all the saints - and for me, that utterance may be given to me, that I may open my mouth boldly to make known the mystery of the gospel, for which I am an ambassador in chains; that in it I may speak boldly, as I ought to speak.

[Ephesians 6:17-20]

Freedom fighters are men of the Word and they are men of prayer. They are people who engage in the application and declaration of Biblical truth and they are people who lifting their voices in prayer to the Father.

True sons love to read and study the Word.

True sons love the secret place of prayer.

Our Beginning and End

Prayer features a great deal in Paul's Letter to the Ephesians. He starts the letter with a prayer of thanksgiving:

Blessed be the God and Father of our Lord Jesus Christ, who has blessed us with every spiritual blessing in the heavenly places in Christ.

[Ephesians 1.3]

He adds that he continually thinks of the congregation in Ephesus and prays for them earnestly:

I also, after I heard of your faith in the Lord Jesus and your love for all the saints, do not cease to give thanks for you, making mention of you in my prayers.

[Ephesians 1.15-16]

In the centre of his letter, Paul returns to the subject of prayer, this time modelling to his spiritual children how they should pray:

I bow my knees to the Father of our Lord Jesus Christ, from whom the whole family in heaven and earth is named, that He would grant you, according to the riches of His glory, to be strengthened with might through His Spirit in the inner man.

[Ephesians 3:14-16]

Now at the conclusion of his letter in Ephesians 6, Paul returns to the subject, urging his readers to watch and pray.

See how prayer lies at the beginning, middle and end of Paul's letter. In Paul's mind, prayer must be the highest priority at the start, the middle and the conclusion of one's tasks. Just as the Jewish man prayed three times each day – at dawn, noon and night – so Paul, in a thoroughly Jewish way, tells us to make sure our lives are begun, sustained and ended in prayer.

Prayer is accordingly a key theme in Paul's letter.

And it is a fitting conclusion to Paul's passage about the spiritual war in Ephesians 6.10-20.

Territory, Weaponry, Strategy

If we look closely at how Paul designs the famous passage on the armour of God in Ephesians 6 we can see that as so often he is thinking in threes.

The start of Paul's call to arms involves a general description of the spiritual battle itself, in Ephesians 6 verses 10-13:

Finally, my brethren, be strong in the Lord and in the power of His might. Put on the whole armour of God, that you may be able to stand against the wiles of the devil. For we do not wrestle against flesh and blood, but against principalities, against powers, against the rulers of the darkness of this age, against spiritual hosts of wickedness in the heavenly places. Therefore take up the whole armour of God, that you may be able to withstand in the evil day, and having done all, to stand.

This is the territory.

The second section (verses 14-16) describes the six main pieces of armour in the Christian soldier's panoply:

Stand therefore, having girded your waist with truth, having put on the breastplate of righteousness, and having shod your feet with the preparation of the gospel of peace; above all, taking the shield of faith with which you will be able to quench all the fiery darts of the wicked one. And take the helmet of salvation, and the sword of the Spirit, which is the word of God.

This is the weaponry.

Now in the third section Paul turns his attention to the subject of prayer as he asks his readers to be watchful and to pray in the Spirit with all kinds of prayer for all the saints (i.e. for all Christian believers) and especially for him in his preaching of the Gospel. He asks specifically for boldness in preaching the Gospel. Put another way, he asks to be given courage in raising the sword of the Spirit and declaring the word of God, the Gospel of peace.

This is the strategy.

Where is our Spear?

In light of the warfare context, it is interesting to ask the question, "Why does Paul not have prayer represented by a piece of the soldier's armour?" He has done this for every other virtue, why not for prayer?'

This becomes even more interesting when we recall that there is one item in the standard Roman armour in Paul's time which is very noticeable for its absence. This is the spear. In Paul's day, the Roman legionary's principal weapon was not in fact his sword but his *pilum* or spear. In his description of the panoply, the Roman historian Polybius spends much more time describing the legionary's spear than his sword. His descriptions enable us to form a picture of this particular weapon. He says that it was like a moderately sized hunting spear with a barbed iron head fixed to the haft with numerous rivets, making it nearly impossible for it to become detached. The legionaries used to throw these *pila* like missiles into the air and towards the ranks of the enemy in front of them, causing carnage. They would then dash into the disorganised and devastated ranks and put their enemies to the sword.

Given that the *pilum* is effectively an airborne missile, it might seem strange that Paul does not follow his exhortation to take the sword with a call to "pick up and hurl the missile of prayer!" Surely this was a golden opportunity to round off his teaching on spiritual warfare with a seventh armour piece (seven in Judaism is the number of perfection, after all).

Why does he not do this?

The answer is intriguing.

If you look closely at Paul's language about prayer in verses 18-20 there is one thing that may strike you: Paul's perspective is wholly positive. In other words, he stresses that we pray FOR not pray AGAINST things. For Paul, prayer is not about counter-acting negative, hostile forces. It is about giving support to positive advances of the Gospel.

In Paul's understanding of intercession, prayer is therefore not about attacking the dark powers and principalities that govern the governments, as it were. It is not a matter of praying against wicked hosts, demonic strongholds or so-called territorial spirits (a phrase that has gained increasing traction in recent years). There is not a single hint anywhere in Paul's writing that prayer consists of throwing metaphorical missiles at the powers. There is no suggestion that we are called to throw intercessory spears at the devil either. Rather, prayer is prayer FOR something, not prayer AGAINST. It is a positive enterprise not a negative one.

The Freedom Fighter's Focus

This is a good place to say something more generally about Paul's admirable way of thinking. The truth is that Paul does not write to his congregations and encourage them to be defined by what they are against. Quite the opposite, he writes and exhorts them to be known by what they are for.

Are you known for what you're against or what you're for?

When it comes to the Roman Emperor for example, Paul nowhere advocates that his spiritual sons and daughters spend their time going around saying that Caesar (i.e. the Emperor) is not Lord. He tells them simply to state the positive – that Jesus Christ is Lord. He stresses what they are for not what they are against.

This mindset is carried over into Paul's practice of prayer. He does not pray against the principalities and powers of the Empire even though these are the dark forces used by the evil one and against which we wrestle. Rather, he teaches us to use prayer in an altogether different way - one that freedom fighters need to apply.

There are three things that are noteworthy about Paul's call to prayer in Ephesians 6.18-20.

The first is that this kind of praying should be **Spirit-led.** The Greek word *pneuma* can be translated 'spirit.' Paul says that we are to pray 'in the Spirit,' (*en peneumati*) referring to the Holy Spirit. The Holy Spirit is in fact the Spirit who prays in and through us

(Romans 8.27). Through the Spirit, we are joined to the intercession of the Son of God at the Father's throne (Romans 8.34). The role of the Holy Spirit can therefore never be underemphasized. Rather than focusing on demonic spirits, Paul focuses on the Holy Spirit. For him it is vital that we yield in our own prayer life to the intercession of the Holy Spirit, whose sighs and groans within us are evidence that we have been connected to the passionate praying of the Son before his loving Father in heaven (Romans 8.26). Spirit-empowered prayer is therefore the priority. We have to earnestly seek the leading of the Holy Spirit whenever we pray.

The second thing to say is that this kind of prayer should be **steadfast**. Paul calls Christian soldiers to engage in watchful and persevering prayer (Colossians 4:2). The Christian soldier keeps the watch and prays. He asks for the anointing of the Holy Spirit and prays without ceasing for the breakthrough in any given situation. He does not falter and he does not quit. He goes on praying as the Spirit guides him until the Spirit says 'it is finished.' In the spiritual battle, prayer – whatever form it takes in any individual's life, intercession or petition (Ephesians 6.18) – must be unrelenting. Perseverance is paramount.

Thirdly, the kind of prayer Paul is talking about needs to be **specific**. In Ephesians 6.18-20 Paul starts with a broad canvas but narrows down to a very precise focus. He begins with a call to intercede 'for all the saints,' – that is, for those who are in Christ on the earth. He then homes in on his own need – the need to preach the Gospel boldly. What really matters is that freedom fighters specifically pray for one another that they are fearless in sharing the Good News about Jesus wherever and whenever a door of opportunity opens for us.

Notice the word translated 'boldly.' It is the Greek word *parresia*. This is exactly the same word that is used by Luke in Acts 4.31. In that passage we find the earliest, persecuted church praying to the Sovereign Lord that he would give them all boldness and that he would also stretch out his hand to perform signs and wonders.

CHAPTER 10 | RAISING A LOUD SHOUT

The answer comes immediately with a dramatic manifestation of the presence of the Spirit and an overwhelming empowering to speak *parresia* or boldly. This in turn launches the church into a new phase of effectiveness in mission as the believers preach the message of the Gospel with miracles.

This is the focus of true intercession. We do not pray against anything or anyone. Instead, we pray for those things that will advance the Good News. We pray for the ability to speak *parresia*, with courage, clarity and conviction.

For that to happen, someone somewhere needs to pray.

Positive Praying

Why, then, does Paul not call us to raise and hurl the spear of prayer?

Why does he not complete the Roman panoply?

The answer is because prayer is not hurling curses against powers, people or places. Rather, prayer is interceding and petitioning in the Spirit for those God-given blessings that will lead to the Gospel being understood, declared, confirmed and advanced in the world.

Prayer is therefore a discipline with a positive focus, something that is visible throughout Ephesians as a whole. Look at what Paul stresses about prayer.

First of all, let's remember that prayer for Paul is about **intimacy**. For him, prayer is loving communion with Abba, Father. Prayer is conversation between adopted sons and daughters and their heavenly Papa. Prayer, as Paul puts it in Ephesians 3.14, is a matter of bowing the knee before the Father. It is about relationship – intimate friendship with Father God, in Christ, through the power of the Holy Spirit. In Christ, everyone can access to Abba, Father (Ephesians 2.18). Paul longs for all of us to understand that prayer is therefore love on its knees. This is why he prays for his congregation in Ephesus that they might come to know the inexhaustible dimensions of the divine love.

This brings us to a second positive focus and that has to do with **insight**. Paul knows that adopted children in the Roman world became the legitimate heirs of their father's estate. Inheritance was therefore a big deal. Newly adopted children found themselves receiving both now and in the future glorious riches that they simply hadn't earned or deserved. For Paul, this idea is carried over into the Christian life. Once we were orphans but now we are sons by adoption and as sons we are heirs - in fact, co-heirs with Jesus. For us to receive the full glory of this inheritance we must have insight into the legacy left to us through the finished work of the Cross. This is why Paul says in Ephesians 1.15-19:

I also, after I heard of your faith in the Lord Jesus and your love for all the saints, do not cease to give thanks for you, making mention of you in my prayers: that the God of our Lord Jesus Christ, the Father of glory, may give to you the spirit of wisdom and revelation in the knowledge of Him, the eyes of your understanding being enlightened; that you may know what is the hope of His calling, what are the riches of the glory of His inheritance in the saints, and what is the exceeding greatness of His power toward us who believe.

See how positive Paul's focus is in these verses! He is praying for not against. He is asking that the adopted sons and daughters of God will know a deeper revelation of their Heavenly Father (that's intimacy) and that they will have a complete grasp of what is theirs in Christ. Here he is praying for insight, insight about the inheritance coming to the believer in the present and future tenses of their lives. This is why in Ephesians 3.17-19 he prays 'that you, being rooted and grounded in love, may be able to comprehend with all the saints what is the width and length and depth and height - to know the love of Christ which passes knowledge; that you may be filled with all the fullness of God.'

But it doesn't end here. Paul has a third positive focus in mind. This we can call **inroads**. Paul believes that prayer is about asking the Father to open up a way for the advance of the Gospel. The man who falls in love with God and begins to marvel at all that he has in Christ cannot help but share such glorious truths with others. This is much too good to be kept to oneself. As a newly adopted son, rescued from a hopeless orphanage, he is desperate to find other spiritual orphans and introduce them to Jesus. He is eager for Abba, Father to make the road straight for sharing the best news in the universe.

You cannot deny that this is positive! Paul's prayer life embraced a cycle of intimacy, insight and inroads. He prayed for his readers to have increasing intimacy because he knew that this would lead to increasing insight which would in turn result inevitably in increasing inroads:

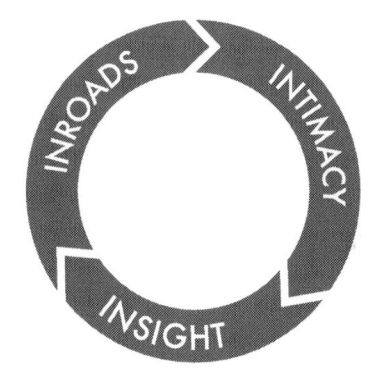

Resurrection Power

Prayer is essential because it opens a freedom fighter up to the empowering presence of God. This is why Paul prays that his readers will come to know "what is the exceeding greatness of His power toward us who believe, according to the working of His mighty power which He worked in Christ when He raised Him from the dead and seated Him at His right hand in the heavenly places, far above all principality and power and might and dominion, and every name that is named, not only in this age but also in that which is to come" (Ephesians 1.19-21).

Positive praying releases a greater awareness of the extraordinary supernatural power available to those who are in Christ. This is the same power that raised Jesus Christ from the dead and elevated him to the throne of God in heaven. This same death-defeating power is available to us as part of our inheritance as adopted sons and daughters. With this power, inroads can be made that are not the product of our own efforts but the result of the resurrection power of God at work. When such power is displayed, spiritual orphans find peace with God and peace with each other. The sick are healed, the oppressed are set free, the poor are blessed and the dead are raised. Instead of an Empire being extended through brute force, the Kingdom of Heaven is advanced through the proclamation and demonstration of the Gospel of peace.

This is a positive vision!

And this is prayer!

Paul begins his letter by saying, 'I'm praying for you.'

He ends it by saying, 'now please pray for me.'

For Paul, even though the world is a battleground not a playground, he doesn't call us to pray against the enemy. He calls us to pray for each other, that we would enjoy increasing intimacy, insight and inroads.

In a church where it is predominantly the daughters of God who travail in prayer, the sons need to catch this vision. Prayer is for men as well as women. And prayer is not throwing spears into the hordes of hell and its Satanic general. It is an intimate communion and loving conversation with our heavenly Father. It is the act in which we receive increasing insight into the mystery of the Gospel and the riches of our inheritance. It is the source of our spiritual power and strength as we stand in the battle. And it is the means by which we call out to the Commander of heaven's army on behalf of a brother or brothers who need reinforcements, supplies, protection or intervention.

CHAPTER 10 | RAISING A LOUD SHOUT

An Armour Dressing Prayer

The Celtic Christians believed in praying what are known as 'dressing prayers.' These prayers were prayed by the Christian as he got up in the morning. One of the best known of these is Saint Patrick's Breastplate from (most likely) the eighth century. This was later transformed into a hymn which begins with the following stanza:

I bind unto myself today

The strong Name of the Trinity,

By invocation of the same

The Three in One and One in Three.

I want to urge you to pray an armour dressing prayer as you make your stand in the spiritual battle, dressed in the panoply of the spiritual legionary.

Here it is. May it lead to many people being set free by the glorious Gospel of our Lord Jesus Christ!

"Dear Lord and heavenly Father,

As a freedom fighter, I commit myself this day to stand firm in the spiritual battle and to remain faithful to your Son, the Lord Jesus Christ.

I bind unto myself the belt of truth, covenanting with you, my heavenly Father, to make the true truth of Jesus Christ central to my life and to be a truthful person and a truth-teller in every circumstance.

I place the breastplate over my chest and dedicate my heart to living in a right relationship with you, to behaving in the righteous way that Jesus would want, and respecting and promoting the rights of the oppressed.

I take the shoes of preparation and put them on my feet, promising to be ready in every situation to turn my armour against the enemy not against my family, my friends or my workmates, and thereby to promote peace.

I place the helmet of salvation on my head and celebrate the wonderful fact that I have been saved from slavery and adopted into the glorious freedom of being a son, and I ask you to renew my mind with this truth.

I receive from you the shield of faith and I believe in my heart and declare with my mouth that Jesus alone is the Son of God, my Lord, Saviour of the world, the Prince of Peace, and the Coming King.

I also receive the sword and promise to speak incisively, under the anointing of the Holy Spirit, about the glorious Good News about Jesus, and how he makes peace between us and God, and between each other, at the Cross.

I commit myself, Abba Father, to standing as a soldier and a son, in the full armour that you provide.

With my brothers in Christ, I vow not to falter or fall today but to be faithful and true to you.

And I ask for the resurrection power of your Holy Spirit so that I may be victorious in every battle as I fight for my own freedom and for the freedom of those enslaved by the enemy.

I make this prayer in the strong name of Jesus Christ, with whom I am seated in the heavenly realms,

Amen.

CHAPTER 10 | RAISING A LOUD SHOUT

APPLYING THE FREEDOM FIGHTING PRINCIPLES

What am I going to *do* in response to what I've read in this chapter?

Action Point 1

Action Point 2

Action Point 3

What am I going to pray for as a result of what I've read?

Prayer Point 1

Prayer Point 2

Prayer Point 3

PERSONAL TRAINING:

Spend some time considering the following.

PERSONAL PRAYER REVIEW:

What level of discipline in prayer do I currently have?

How much do I focus on intimacy with the Father?

Is my focus negative or positive?

To what extent do I pray strategically for the advance of the Gospel?

In what ways do I allow the Holy Spirit to lead my praying?

How am I going to change the way I pray from now on?

CHAPTER 10 | RAISING A LOUD SHOUT

GROUP TRAINING:

CORPORATE PRAYER REVIEW:

To what extent do you support one another in prayer?

Are you watching each others' backs in prayer?

Are you seeking to win spiritual battles by praying positively or praying negatively?

What healthy, Biblical prayer tactics do you now need to develop as a group?

How can you use the freedom fighter's dressing prayer as you intercede together?

In what ways can your collective praying become more Spirit-led?

FREEDOM FIGHTERS

Printed in Poland
by Amazon Fulfillment
Poland Sp. z o.o., Wrocław